DYNAMIC PSYCHOTHERAPY WITH THE BORDERLINE PATIENT

William N. Goldstein, M.D.

to Bob
an outstanding psychiatrist,
analyst, and friend.
Bill

JASON ARONSON INC.
Northvale, New Jersey
London

This book was set in 11 point Bem by TechType of Ramsey, New Jersey and printed and bound by Book-mart Press of North Bergen, New Jersey.

10 9 8 7 6 5 4 3 2 1

Library of Congress Cataloging-in-Publication Data

Goldstein, William N.
Dynamic psychotherapy with the borderline patient / William N. Goldstein.
p. cm.
Includes bibliographical references and index.
ISBN 1-56821-817-6
1. Borderline personality disorder—Treatment. 2. Psychotherapy.
I. Title.
[DNLM: 1. Borderline Personality Disorder—diagnosis.
2. Borderline Personality Disorder—therapy. 3. Borderline Personality Disorder—psychology. WM 190 G624p 1996]
RC569.5.B67G656 1995
616.85'85—dc20
DNLM/DLC
for Library of Congress 96-4641

Manufactured in the United States of America. Jason Aronson Inc. offers books and cassettes. For information and catalog write to Jason Aronson Inc., 230 Livingston Street, Northvale, New Jersey 07647.

Contents

PART II: PSYCHOTHERAPY

PART III: TECHNIQUE

Acknowledgment

I would like to thank Ms. Flora Paoli for her consistent support and her outstanding typing skills. Her efforts made my work much easier. I would also like to thank Martin Ceaser, M.D., for his helpful review of several chapters and Boyd Burris, M.D., for his positive influence in my decision to finally write a second book.

Introduction

Borderline individuals are generally acknowledged to be among the most confusing, anxiety-provoking, and difficult psychotherapy patients. Yet increasingly they are seeking treatment, both in mental health clinics and private offices. This book presents a psychodynamically based psychotherapy for these patients. A major goal is to present a clear, practical, and useful guide to doing this type of psychotherapy. This book is written especially for mental health professionals who are not completely at home working with borderline patients. Yet it also provides a useful reference and approach for more experienced therapists.

Because there continues to be confusion about the term *borderline,* and because a theoretical framework and background are indispensable for doing psychotherapy with borderline patients, Part I of the book provides a psychodynamic overview. The first four chapters, in particular, provide a very usable framework regarding diagnosis, differential diagnosis, psychodynamics, and prognosis. The next three chapters, on projective identification, the depressive impulse-ridden character and the core borderline personality, and different concepts of the borderline patient, are more specialized, providing additional clarification regarding the borderline concept.

Part II presents an overview of psychotherapy with the borderline patient. Five types of psychotherapy along a continuum from most insight-oriented to most supportive are examined: psychoanalysis, analytically oriented psychotherapy, modified analytically oriented psychotherapy, dynamically oriented psychotherapy, and supportive psychotherapy. Treatment of the borderline patient is then discussed in accordance with each of these classifications. Because of the overwhelming influence and relevance of Kernberg, Adler, and Meissner to my work, I have devoted separate short chapters to each of these experts. As an example of a more supportive but very reasonable approach, I have also devoted a separate short chapter to Rockland. Additionally the work of Giovacchini; Abend, Porder, and Willick; Masterson and Rinsley; and Zetzel is reviewed. Reference is made to the work of Gunderson, Stone, Chessick, Volkan, and Grinker.

Part III presents my ideas regarding psychotherapy and therapeutic technique. This section is filled with clinical vignettes. It begins by presenting an overall strategy and framework for dealing with borderline patients. Emphasis is on the borderline patient's typical problem with forming and maintaining a therapeutic alliance. Because of this problem, much of the early therapeutic work focuses on issues concerning the alliance. Meaningful interventions regarding core difficulties (other than those involving the alliance) can only occur when there is a workable therapeutic alliance. Typically there is an oscillation between focus on the therapeutic alliance and interventions involving other core difficulties. Unending sequences occur, with disruption of the therapeutic alliance, followed by interventions that strengthen the alliance, followed by interventions regarding other core difficulties, followed by other disruptions, and so forth. To minimize disruptions, interventions are delivered in an empathic and affirmative way, with preparatory comments and with input from the patient. Techniques regarding the above forms of interventions are addressed in a subsequent chapter. In psychotherapy with the most favorable outcome, the therapeutic alliance, very gradually and incrementally, becomes increasingly stable, and the therapeutic focus shifts more and more to interventions regarding the other core difficulties.

Rapid mobilization of the transference is typical of the borderline patient in the early phase of psychotherapy. One group of patients uses the transference throughout the treatment as the main modality through which conflicts unfold and are resolved. A second group, after much initial difficulty, maintains a relatively stable therapeutic alliance and then uses that alliance as a vehicle to explore conflicts outside of the transference. Focus in this group is on the core difficulties as they play out in the workplace and with spouses, friends, and acquaintances. The first group uses what I will call a modified analytically oriented approach throughout the course of psychotherapy. The second group starts with an analytically oriented approach; then, after the establishment of a reasonable therapeutic alliance, switches to what I call a dynamically oriented modality.

Separate chapters describe interventions regarding the core difficulties. These include anxiety and defense, primitive defenses, severe acting out, introjects, and reality testing. Although anxiety and defense are listed as a separate category, there is a preference for utilizing this conceptual framework when making any intervention. Regarding interventions, both insight-oriented and supportive techniques are reviewed. Usually insight-oriented interventions are attempted first. Whenever these are insufficient, they are complemented or supplanted by more supportive techniques. Whenever reasonable, movement is toward the insight-oriented interventions. It is the preponderance of the insight-oriented versus supportive interventions that determines the overall coloring of the therapy. Some borderline patients do well with a primarily insight-oriented approach; others need more supportive mechanisms.

In addition to the above, larger issues regarding psychotherapy are examined. These include the stability of the therapeutic environment, the neutrality and flexibility of the therapist, the countertransference, the activity of the therapist, and the mechanism of change in psychotherapy. A chapter is devoted to the arrangements of psychotherapy, including scheduling, lateness, interactions outside the therapy hours, payments, missed appointments, guidelines for the patient, and contracts. There are separate chapters on the therapeutic alliance and the transference, and on phases, trends, and termination.

Part I

PSYCHODYNAMICS

1

DIAGNOSIS

HISTORICAL BACKGROUND

The term *borderline* first appeared in the psychoanalytic literature in the mid-1900s, only later to become a generally used term among psychiatrists and other mental health professionals. Early on, analysts were confronted with the situation in which a patient came for analysis, seemed analyzable, but when on the couch proved to have great difficulties with the process. Obviously the patient was much more disturbed than originally thought. As different analysts had different negative experiences with these types of patients, they wrote papers using different terms to describe these more troubled individuals. The early psychoanalytic papers on the borderline patient fall into two groups. One group views these patients as having a mild form of schizophrenia, whereas a second group views them as a distinct and separate group of individuals, neither neurotic nor psychotic, operating psychopathologically on a level between the two. Many of the patients from both of these groups would be considered borderline today.

The first group includes the ambulatory schizophrenic of Zilboorg (1941), the pseudoneurotic schizophrenic of Hoch and Polatin (1949), the latent psychotic of Bychowsky (1953), and the pseudopsychopathic schizophrenic of Dunaif and Hoch (1955). Zilboorg coined the term *ambulatory schizophrenia,* to refer to a group of patients whom he considered to have mild schizophrenia, but who could function in day-to-day living without the need for hospitalization. Hoch and Polatin used the term *pseudoneurotic schizophrenia* to refer to a group of patients that basically looked neurotic, but under close scrutiny turned out to be schizophrenic. The traits of pananxiety, pansexuality, and panneurosis were characteristic of this group. Analogously, a group of pseudopsychopathic schizophrenic patients was later described by Dunaif and Hoch. Bychowsky used the term *latent psychosis* to refer to a group of patients who had a great potential to regress and become psychotic under severe stress.

The second group includes the borderline of Stern (1938), the as-if personality of Deutsch (1942), the borderline of Knight (1953), and the psychotic character of Frosch (1964). Stern was the first to use the term *borderline* formally, describing ten diagnostic criteria for making the diagnosis. He was also the first to conceptualize this group of patients as having a kind of stable psychopathology, somewhere between neurosis and psychosis in severity. In this regard, he predated Kernberg by a number of years. Deutsch offered the term *as-if personality* for a group of patients who functioned as if they were normal, but who under close scrutiny revealed clear pathology in their internalized object relations. These individuals acted in a chameleon-like way, becoming part of whatever group with which they had contact, then readily and rapidly shifting alliances when the next group presented itself.

Knight also used the term *borderline,* here to refer to a group of patients who, from an ego-psychological point of view, displayed similarities to both neurotic and psychotic patients. Emphasizing the weakening of ego functions in these patients, he viewed this group as midline between neurosis and psychosis. Frosch coined the term *psychotic character* to refer again to patients of an intermediate range of psychopathology. Although these patients shared many ego-psychological characteristics with psychotics, they differed from psychotic patients in their relative ability to preserve reality testing, their superior object relations, and their capacity for reversibility if and when they did regress. Rapaport, Gill, and Schafer (1945–1946), from the world of psychological testing, complemented these works by describing a group of preschizophrenic patients who, on psychological testing, revealed a predominance of primary-process thinking and a generalized weakening of ego functioning as compared to more neurotic patients.

In 1967 Otto Kernberg wrote his seminal paper, providing for many an integration and synthesis of all earlier writings on the borderline patient, and offering a unified and comprehensive framework for description, definition, and understanding. Although he elaborated, updated, and modified his original article, contributing many additional ideas regarding the borderline patient (1975, 1976, 1980, 1984), his core ideas are still expressed in his 1967 paper. For some, Kernberg's writings, characterized by terminology and language related to an underlying sophisticated psychoanalytic object relations theory with Kleinian influence, are too difficult and confusing. Despite this, his work remains central to current psychoanalytic thinking regarding the borderline patient. With this in mind I wrote (Goldstein 1982, 1985, 1987, 1988b, 1989b, 1995) a number of papers presenting Kernberg's work in a more simplified fashion. I used the term *ego-psychological diagnostic approach* to describe a way of dynamically presenting the borderline patient based on a profile of ego strengths and ego weaknesses. This ego-psychological diagnostic approach is based on Kernberg's ideas, but it simplifies and sometimes modifies his work, and additionally includes aspects of the borderline patient not stressed by him.

I think this approach provides a current summary of the psychodynamic concept of the borderline individual.

THE EGO-PSYCHOLOGICAL DIAGNOSTIC APPROACH

The borderline patient has a specific stable pathological personality organization characterized by a specific kind of underlying structural configuration. This structural configuration includes a distinct kind of ego and superego functioning and a distinct pattern of instinctual drive organization. This configuration is quite stable and resistant to change, except through intensive psychotherapeutic intervention or with the passage of much time. The borderline patient is viewed as having one of four structural configurations, within which all patients can be classified diagnostically. Thus, the borderline structural configuration, along with the normal-neurotic, the narcissistic, and the psychotic, provide first-level or supraordinate "structural" diagnoses under which all other descriptive diagnoses fall. Although the structural configuration includes a specific kind of ego and superego functioning, as well as a specific pattern of instinctual drive organization, the focus for diagnostic purposes is largely on the ego.

Relying on the model of Beres (1956) and Bellak (1958), the borderline patient's ego is viewed in accordance with the various ego functions. The borderline individual is thus described as having a particular ego structure, consisting of a specific pattern of relative ego strengths and underlying ego weaknesses.

The relative ego strengths are as follows:

1. the relative intactness of reality testing,
2. the relative intactness of thought processes,
3. the relative intactness of interpersonal relations,
4. the relative intactness of the adaptation to reality.

It must be stressed that these four strengths are only relative; they easily break down to various degrees in various situations. Because these four relative strengths stand out superficially, they enable the borderline individual to present a fairly "normal" appearance. These relative strengths, particularly the first two, most clearly differentiate the borderline from the more psychotic individual.

The underlying ego weaknesses are as follows:

1. the combination of poor impulse control and poor frustration tolerance,
2. the proclivity to use primitive ego defenses,
3. the syndrome of identity diffusion,
4. affective instability.

In contrast to the strengths, which stand out on a superficial level, these weaknesses only become clearly apparent with in-depth understanding. Except during regressed states, a detailed history or a relationship over time is needed for these weaknesses to emerge clearly. Because these weaknesses are beneath the surface and are not detected superficially, they do not detract from the borderline's appearance of normality. These underlying weaknesses, however, most clearly differentiate the borderline from the more neurotic individual. A brief look at the relative ego strengths and underlying ego weaknesses will now be undertaken.

The Relative Ego Strengths

In discussing the four relative ego strengths, emphasis will be on both the strengths and the weaknesses regarding each ego function.

Reality Testing

The strength here is that, on a surface level, and in day-to-day functioning, reality testing is basically intact. The weakness can emerge under stress and in very close interpersonal situations where there is a tendency for this ego function to regress, sometimes leading to brief psychotic episodes. Regarding symptomatology, it is sometimes difficult to differentiate these regressions from other psychotic episodes. What does distinguish these episodes is their brevity (minutes up to a day or two), their spontaneous reversibility, and their relationship to clear-cut precipitating events. These transient psychotic episodes under stress are allowable but certainly not mandatory to making the diagnosis of borderline.

Thought Processes

The strength is that, in day-to-day functioning and in structured situations, thought processes are predominantly secondary process. The weakness can come about under stress and in unstructured situations (such as projective psychological testing) when primary process sometimes emerges. Although there is the tendency to find a psychological test pattern of secondary process on the WAIS and primary process on the Rorschach, there is much disagreement as to how frequently this test pattern will actually be found in the borderline patient. The feeling here is that, although the finding of secondary process on the WAIS and primary process on the Rorschach is presumptive evidence for the borderline diagnosis, this pattern is clearly not necessary for making the diagnosis.

Interpersonal Relations

The strength here is that the borderline patient often seems to do adequately in interpersonal relations. On the surface he seems to "relate" to others, can have many acquaintances, and sometimes can even maintain long-term relationships. Weaknesses in this area emerge when, under closer scrutiny, it becomes apparent that the relationships are often characterized by a striking lack of depth and a lack of concern for the other individual as a person. The other person is seen as someone who can be used to meet the borderline patient's needs rather than as a person in his own right. Depth and empathy are lacking, and the borderline individual often vacillates between superficial relationships and intense, dependent relationships that are marred by primitive defenses. In his relationships, the borderline patient is often very sensitive to real or imagined abandonments and to real or perceived slights, rejections, rebuffs, disappointments, and failures. The terms *need-fulfilling relations, as-if relationships, relationships based on part objects,* and *selfobject relationships* are all relevant here.

Adaptation to Reality

The strength here is that adaptation to reality is often superficially intact. The borderline patient may seem of normal appearance and may seem to display adequate achievement in work or school. Weaknesses in this area emerge when, under closer scrutiny, there is often a feeling that the adaptation is far from optimal. There are certain "exceptional" borderlines who can maximize certain strengths and adapt adequately over time, particularly in structured settings. These individuals often do quite well professionally, while typically displaying much more chaos in their social lives. Typically, these people display certain marked ego strengths together with their weaknesses. Strengths often include high intelligence and the ability to use obsessive compulsive defenses. This exceptional group, more than others, seeks out intensive psychotherapy.

We will now turn to the underlying ego weaknesses.

The Underlying Ego Weaknesses

Poor Impulse Control and Poor Frustration Tolerance

Invariably, the borderline patient displays the combination of poor frustration tolerance and poor impulse control. There is an inability to delay, a demand for immediate gratification, and a proclivity to act out under stress. To make matters more difficult, these characteristics are frequently combined with a sense of entitlement. These difficulties most frequently present themselves clinically by a tendency for states of disruptive anger, by the use of drugs and alcohol to avoid frustration and obtain temporary gratification, and by an inclination to flee the work or interpersonal situation under stress. There is a tendency in some for impulsive suicidal threats and attempts, in addition to other self-destructive behavior.

The Proclivity to Use Primitive Ego Defenses

Emphasis here is on the *proclivity* to use primitive ego defenses. The borderline patient does not use primitive defenses all the time. In day-to-day functioning, he tends to use primitive defenses somewhat more than the neurotic; under stress, he tends to rely on these defenses. Following Vaillant (1971), one can classify defenses into a hierarchy of five levels of increasing psychopathology: mature, neurotic, immature, borderline, and psychotic. With this hierarchy in mind, these generalizations can be made. In day-to-day functioning, the borderline patient, with marked individual variation, uses a combination of mature, neurotic, immature, and borderline defenses. Under stress, he displays a marked tendency to rely on the borderline defenses. In marked regressions, he may also use some psychotic defenses. Borderline defenses include splitting, primitive idealization, projection, projective identification, primitive denial, omnipotence, and devaluation. These are the defenses considered by Kernberg to be pathognomonic. Primitive defenses are thought to include, in addition to the above, acting out and the psychotic defenses.

Splitting refers to the tendency to view individuals and things (external objects) as either all-good or all-bad. Primitive idealization, devaluation, and omnipotence are viewed as derivatives of splitting. Primitive idealization is the positive component of the split directed toward an external object (or individual). The external object is viewed as all-good not for any realistic reason, but because the patient has the need or wish to see it as all-good. Devaluation is the negative component of the split, directed toward an external object or toward the self. Omnipotence is the positive component of the split directed toward the self. Although many patients make rapid reversals from one side of the split to the other, particularly under stress, others tend to maintain their primitive idealizations and devaluations over long periods of time.

The denial characteristic of most borderline patients is of a primitive, global, and blatantly unrealistic nature, somewhat akin to splitting. Two events or facts are clearly remembered in consciousness, yet one is totally denied or ignored. Alternatively, an event or fact is clearly remembered, but there is total disregard of its implications, consequences, and relevance.

Projective identification is the most confusing of all the borderline defenses. One does not need to use the term *projective identification*; one can use other language to describe the same phenomenon. However, this term has become commonplace, and it behooves one to understand it. The most common usage of projective identification is as follows. A projection is followed by an interpersonal interaction in which the projector actively pressures the recipient to think, feel, and act in accordance with the projection. It is this coercive interpersonal interaction that is the essential feature of projective identification. What is confusing about the term is the varying definitions of projection, whether the process must include a blurring of self and object representations, and whether a reinternalization process (occurring after the interpersonal interaction) should be part of the concept. Elaboration of this concept will be undertaken in Chapter 5 on "Projective Identification."

Identity Diffusion

This term refers to an identity that is not integrated or cohesive, but diffuse. It is an identity based on multiple contradictory unintegrated self images. Correspondingly, there are multiple contradictory unintegrated object images. At one time one self image is evoked, at another time, a different one. This same applies to object images. Neither a comprehensive view of the self nor of objects has ever been attained. Because of this, the borderline individual is unable to describe himself or others in a meaningful way. There is a lack of temporal continuity regarding the self and others, along with an overall distortion of the perceptions of self and others. Sometimes the borderline patient experiences an inner lack or void, a sense of emptiness or depletion. Various types of stimulating activities, including self-mutilating behaviors, are sometimes used to get rid of these painful feelings. Other terms frequently used to describe this problem include the lack of an integrated self concept, a lack of a sense of self, the lack of a real self, the lack of a stable identity, and the lack of a coherent sense of self.

Affective Instability

Irritability; intense affect, usually depressive or hostile; anger as the main affect experienced; and depressed, lonely, and empty feelings are frequently emphasized. Aggression is not utilized in constructive, ego-syntonic, adaptive ways, such as sublimations, work, recreation, and enjoyment. Psychoanalytically, this characteristic is related to a defect in the neutralization of aggression. Thus, the aggression often breaks through directly in disruptive ways, such as outbursts of anger and rage; or the aggression is defended against in maladaptive ways and results in other ego-dystonic affect states, such as depression, boredom, and emptiness. Often there can be rapid and dramatic swings from one affect state to another.

USE OF THE EGO-PSYCHOLOGICAL DIAGNOSTIC APPROACH

In using the ego-psychological diagnostic approach, one does not need to demonstrate all four ego strengths and all four ego weaknesses to make the diagnosis. In contrast, one looks at the overall pattern of ego strengths and weaknesses and establishes into which large grouping (the normal-neurotic, the narcissistic, the borderline, or the psychotic) the patient best fits. The borderline concept outlined here is quite broad. It can be thought of as including a heterogeneous group of patients with varying degrees of pathological functioning, various personality styles, and various symptoms. What differentiates this heterogeneous group from the other large groupings is the underlying pattern of ego strengths and ego weaknesses just elaborated.

THE WORK OF MEISSNER

The ego-psychological diagnostic approach is thought to complement the work of Meissner (1982–1983, 1983, 1984) regarding the borderline spectrum. I agree with Meissner, who views the borderline conditions as consisting of a heterogeneous group of patients represented by a spectrum of levels and degrees of pathological personality functioning. Meissner takes the ego-psychological diagnostic approach a step further by dividing borderline patients into two large groupings: the hysterical continuum and the schizoid continuum. Each continuum is subdivided into different diagnostic categories, according to degree of psychopathology. The different categories are differentiated by several parameters, including the quality of object relations, the degree of object constancy, the level of achieved and maintained self-cohesion, the regressive potential, the degree of projective tendency, and the levels of ego and superego structuralization. Although different in detail, these differentiating parameters are like those of the ego-psychological diagnostic approach.

DSM-IV

DSM-IV (1994) is the current official nomenclature, generally used and accepted in psychiatry today. It is an atheoretical and totally descriptive approach, devoid of any psychodynamic underpinnings. Regarding the borderline patient, it represents a culmination of a series of approaches emphasizing a description that is easily defined, reliable, and valid. These approaches followed the psychodynamic, and in part were in response to concern about the variability of the descriptions of the psychodynamic group. Using literature reviews, research designs, and statistical methods, attempts were undertaken to identify those traits and symptoms that differentiated the borderline patient from other diagnostic groups. The work of Gunderson and colleagues (1975), Gunderson and Singer (1975), and Gunderson and Kolb (1978), and of Perry and Klerman (1978, 1980) are the best known of these approaches prior to the task force of Spitzer and colleagues (1979), leading to *DSM-III* (1980).

To make the *DSM-IV* diagnosis of borderline personality disorder, there needs to be a "pervasive pattern of instability of interpersonal relationships, self-image, and affects, and marked impulsivity beginning in early adulthood and present in a variety of contexts." One must demonstrate at least five of nine items on a checklist to establish the diagnosis. These items include (1) frantic efforts to avoid real or imagined abandonment, (2) a pattern of unstable and intense interpersonal relationships characterized or alternating between extremes of idealization and devaluation, (3) identity disturbance, (4) impulsivity in at least two areas that are potentially self-damaging, (5) recurrent suicidal behavior, gestures, or self-mutilating behavior, (6) affective instability due to marked reactivity of mood, (7) chronic feelings of emptiness, (8) inappropriate, intense anger or difficulty controlling anger, and (9) transient, stress-related paranoid ideation or severe dissociative symptoms.

DSM-IV views the borderline patient as one of many personality disorders. Conversely, the ego-psychological diagnostic approach views the borderline individual as characterized by a structural configuration, to be differentiated from three other configurations: the normal-neurotic, the narcissistic, and the psychotic. According to this approach, the borderline configuration is seen as a supraordinate diagnosis, under which more specific personality disorders fall. Although the ego-psychological diagnostic approach, with its psychodynamic underpinnings, is different in theoretical focus from *DSM-IV,* it is clearly compatible with this most commonly used system. All items on the *DSM-IV* diagnostic checklist correspond to the list of ego strengths and ego weaknesses of the ego-psychological diagnostic approach. *DSM-IV* is a more descriptive and atheoretical diagnostic system, more conducive to psychological research. The ego-psychological diagnostic approach, by contrast, is more conducive to understanding and psychotherapeutic intervention.

2

DIFFERENTIAL DIAGNOSIS

This chapter focuses on differential diagnosis in accordance with the four supraordinate structural configurations: the normal-neurotic, the narcissistic, the borderline, and the psychotic. Each of these structural configurations is characterized by a specific pattern of ego and superego functioning along with a specific pattern of instinctual drive organization. The pattern of ego functioning, described as a profile or inventory of ego functions, by itself is sufficient to establish a differential diagnosis among the four configurations. A first-line diagnosis made in accordance with these large groupings provides information invaluable for conceptual understanding, prognostic considerations, and therapeutic planning.

Even with the use of the most elaborate diagnostic systems, many individuals remain difficult to diagnose. Many people simply do not fit clearly into one category or another. There will be many individuals who will be on the "border" between borderline and neurotic, between borderline and narcissistic, or between borderline and psychotic. Furthermore, each of the large diagnostic groupings will contain a great variety of people, with widely different personalities and widely different behaviors.

THE BORDERLINE PATIENT

Using the ego-psychological diagnostic approach, the borderline patient has been presented as having an ego profile characterized by four relative ego strengths and four underlying ego weaknesses. A detailed look at the entire ego profile is of most value when making a differential diagnosis. The relative ego strengths, however, especially reality testing and thought processes, are most helpful in differentiating the borderline from the more psychotic individual. Analogously, the underlying weaknesses, especially the proclivity to use primitive ego defenses and the syndrome of identity diffusion, are most helpful in differentiating the borderline from the basically neurotic individual. The narcissistic individual is differentiated from the borderline by a subtly yet distinctly different ego profile, focusing on identity, impulse control/frustration tolerance, and affective instability.

THE BORDERLINE PATIENT AND THE PSYCHOTIC

In differentiating the borderline patient from the psychotic, the prime focus is on reality testing. The borderline individual is characterized by basically intact reality testing, but with a vulnerability to regress in this area under stress. It is the "usual" intactness that differentiates the borderline patient from the psychotic. The psychotic is characterized by a more constant and global defect in reality testing. Although the difference between the borderline individual and the psychotic in reality testing is usually obvious, difficulties can arise with some psychotic individuals who are able to conceal their problems. These individuals continuously expend energy to prevent distortions in reality testing from surfacing. They only occasionally show psychotic symptoms as they use their resources to fend off the psychoses. Thus they can be difficult to differentiate from borderline individuals who show psychotic symptoms under stress.

A focus on thought processes can also be useful in differentiating the borderline patient from the psychotic. The borderline individual typically uses secondary process thinking but sometimes shows a vulnerability to regress to primary process thinking either under stress or in unstructured situations. A more consistent use of primary process thinking indicates a psychotic process, although many psychotic patients do not show this pattern. Additionally, the psychotic patient typically shows more problems than the borderline individual in both interpersonal relations and adaptation to reality. Like the borderline patient, this patient typically shows poor impulse control and poor frustration tolerance, problems in identity, and affective instability. The usual defensive pattern of the psychotic individual includes a combination of neurotic, immature, borderline, and psychotic defenses in day-to-day functioning, with a proclivity to the use of psychotic defenses under stress.

THE BORDERLINE PATIENT AND THE NEUROTIC

The underlying ego weaknesses are most helpful in differentiating the borderline individual from the neurotic. Among these weaknesses, the tendency to use primitive ego defenses and the syndrome of identity diffusion are of most importance. The neurotic uses mainly neurotic and mature defenses in day-to-day functioning, accentuating certain specific neurotic defenses under stress. There may be some acting out and occasional borderline defenses under stress, but otherwise there is little use of lower-level defenses. This typical pattern is in clear contrast to that of the borderline patient, who has a much greater propensity to use the borderline defenses, both in day-to-day functioning and under stress. Additionally, the neurotic presents a clearly integrated, cohesive, and stable sense of self and a similarly integrated, cohesive, and stable sense of objects. Others are viewed as complex individuals, clearly having needs and desires of their own. Thus, the syndrome of identity diffusion is absent in the neurotic.

In essence, the basically neurotic individual is characterized by intact reality testing, secondary process thinking, good interpersonal relations, good adaptation to reality, good impulse control and frustration tolerance, defenses typically characterized as neurotic or higher level, a stable identity, and affective stability. The level of interpersonal relations and adaptation to reality may vary somewhat. In addition, there can be some slippage in frustration tolerance and impulse control, as well as in affective stability. Marked deviation in any of these areas should call into question the diagnosis of neurosis.

THE BORDERLINE PATIENT AND THE NARCISSISTIC

The differentiation of the borderline patient and the narcissistic, along with the issue of whether the narcissistic individual is a subgroup of the borderline, remains controversial. The two predominant experts on narcissistic personalities, Kernberg and Kohut, are not in agreement here. Kohut (1966, 1968, 1971, 1977) classifies the borderline patient with the psychotic and clearly differentiates this group from the narcissistic personality. Kernberg (1970, 1974, 1975, 1980), in contrast, divides the narcissistic personality into three groups, one of which clearly falls into the borderline category and two of which do not. Although it is true that a number of individuals diagnosed as narcissistic personalities do fall into the borderline group, there appears to be a group of narcissistic patients with ego profiles somewhat similar to the borderline, yet subtly but distinctly different under close scrutiny. This group of individuals includes both Kohut's narcissistic personalities and Kernberg's "healthier" narcissistic personalities. It is this group of individuals that fits into the narcissistic structural configuration. The narcissistic configuration falls between the neurotic and borderline in degree of psychopathology.

The main differences between patients with the narcissistic structural configuration and those with the borderline are in the areas of identity diffusion, impulse control/frustration tolerance, and affective instability. Regarding identity, instead of an unintegrated and unstable identity (identity diffusion), the narcissistic patient has an integrated although pathological identity based on a grandiose self. This identity, although clearly pathological, is basically stable and cohesive and resists disruptive fragmentation.

Regarding impulse control/frustration tolerance and stability of affects, these ego functions are relatively stronger in the narcissistic patient than in the borderline, yet still sensitive to regression. This sensitivity is not global, as with the borderline individual, but is limited to the area of narcissistic vulnerability. Narcissistic patients have highly labile self-esteem. They are exceedingly sensitive to perceived slights, rejections, rebuffs, disappointments, and failures. Reactions to these perceived threats are commonly seen both within and without the therapy hour. The slights, no matter how subtle, often produce very uncomfortable feelings, along with disruptive behavior. The patient may become bored or depressed, feel dull and empty, begin to do his work without vigor or zest, lose his initiative, begin to brood, or become preoccupied with his body. Sometimes he may experience embarrassment, shame, humiliation, or rage. It is especially in regard to those affects that compensatory defenses may ensue. These include various kinds of stimulating and dangerous acting out behavior, perverse sexuality, drug and alcohol abuse. To this pronounced sensitivity to slights and rejections, with the corresponding onset of very uncomfortable feelings and disruptive behavior, is assigned the name *narcissistic vulnerability.*

Regarding the other ego functions, there are fewer differences between narcissistic and borderline patients. Interpersonal relations, intact superficially, are maintained to a somewhat better degree in the narcissistic patient, yet are nonetheless distorted by narcissistic configurations. Reality testing and adaptation to reality are a little better than in the borderline patient, whereas thought processes remain intact. Defenses used by the narcissistic personality can be similar to those employed by borderline individuals. They include primitive idealization, omnipotence, devaluation, and splitting.

THE BORDERLINE PATIENT, *DSM-IV,* AND THE PERSONALITY DISORDERS

The concept of the borderline patient emphasized in this book is that of a supraordinate, or first-level, diagnostic group, under which a number of more specific diagnoses fall. The borderline group is differentiated by its distinct underlying structural configuration from three other large groups—the normal-neurotic, the psychotic, and the narcissistic. This diagnostic approach is in contrast to the more descriptive approach of *DSM-IV* (1994), which views the borderline group as one of a number of distinct personality disorders and attempts to differentiate the borderline category from the other personality disorders. Many problems arise when this latter task is undertaken; in essence, this differentiation often cannot be made adequately.

In accordance with the ego-psychological diagnostic approach, many personality disorders, along with some of the symptomatic neuroses, fall within the borderline group. Included here are most impulse-ridden characters, most inadequate personalities, some schizoid personalities, some narcissistic personalities, some phobic individuals, most paranoid personalities, and most antisocial personalities. Some alcoholics and many drug abusers fall into the borderline group. A number of the personality disorders of *DSM-IV* can be considered part of the borderline group. These include many of the paranoid, schizotypal, histrionic, schizoid, narcissistic, and antisocial personalities.

In accordance with the orientation of this book, this chapter on differential diagnoses is presented in regard to structural configurations. Other aspects of differential diagnoses are not elaborated here. Areas of interest include the relationship of the borderline patient to depression, schizophrenia, organicity, and adolescence.

3

DEVELOPMENTAL PSYCHODYNAMICS

Regarding developmental and etiological theory, this chapter compares and contrasts what I find to be the two most helpful models regarding the borderline patient (Goldstein 1989a). I am referring to the theories of Kernberg (1967, 1975, 1976, 1980, 1984) and Adler (Adler 1981, 1985, Adler and Buie 1979, Buie and Adler 1982–1983). Kernberg's writings (1967, 1975, 1976, 1980, 1984) on the borderline patient have had an unparalleled influence in the mental health world. In fact these writings are mainly responsible for popularizing the term *borderline.* Kernberg's work provides a thorough, in-depth, systematic, and comprehensive overview, integrating and synthesizing all earlier psychodynamic writings. In more recent years Adler (Adler 1981, 1985, Adler and Buie 1979, Buie and Adler 1982–1983) has published an influential volume that challenges Kernberg by presenting a different conceptual framework and positing a different core problem for borderline individuals. To some clinicians, Adler presents a decidedly different focus.

Kernberg believes that the core problem in borderline

patients is the difficulty in integrating positive and negative introjects, with the corresponding failure to attain libidinal object constancy. Adler, in contrast, believes that the core problem of these patients is the inability to establish adequately a specific kind of positive introject, the holding introject. Adler has labeled Kernberg's theory an "ambivalence" theory and called his own a theory of "insufficiency." Others (Waldinger 1987) have taken a step beyond this by contrasting Kernberg's "conflict" theory with that of Adler's "deficit" model.

I content that contraposition of the theories of Kernberg and Adler is erroneous. In the final analysis, Kernberg and Adler subscribe to theories that involve both conflict and deficit. This chapter will show that, despite a number of differences, the theories of Kernberg and Adler are compatible, and in fact can be combined into one integrated model. This model emphasizes two core problems for the borderline individual: (1) the deficiency in holding introjects, and (2) the difficulty in integrating positive and negative introjects. Clinically, this integrated model is applicable to virtually all borderline patients. I first summarize and compare Kernberg's and Adler's theoretical views; then I propose an integrated model supported by several clinical examples.

KERNBERG'S THEORETICAL MODEL

In understanding development, Kernberg utilizes an object relations theory, clearly presented in his second book (1976). He uses the term *self* and *object images* synonymously with *self* and *object representations,* and views these images or representations as occurring shortly after birth. Kernberg hypothesizes that normally developing infants organize their experiences, beginning at about 1 month, according to affect states, initially all-good or all-bad. At first self and object images are fused, and linked with either positive or negative affects. With time there is a linkage of discrete units of self images, discrete units of object images, and discrete affect states. Gradually these units evolve into more complex psychic structure. Mahler (Mahler et al. 1975) provides a widely acceptable developmental model, to which Kernberg's object relations theory can be transposed and more easily understood. Although Kernberg (1980, 1981, 1984) originally utilized a different timetable from Mahler, he is now accepting of her developmental model.

Mahler postulates that during the early months of life, the child goes through an autistic phase (of approximately 1 month) during which he is oblivious to anything except himself, followed by a symbiotic phase (up to around 5 to 10 months) in which he views his mother (or primary love object) as an extension of himself. This is followed by a separation-individuation phase (lasting up to age 2 or 3 years) in which the child gradually differentiates and separates himself from his mother and begins to establish his identity as a person in his own right. It is only at the completion of this stage that the child attains libidinal object constancy, the ability to maintain a relative nonchanging emotional image of others as being basically good but having both good and bad qualities, an emotional image that changes little under frustration or during absence.

It is around the transition from the symbiotic to the separation-individuation phase that the child develops stranger anxiety, as has been eloquently described by Spitz (1965). This momentous accomplishment, the ability of the child to distinguish himself from his mother, is synonymous with the child's acquiring the capacity to test reality and corresponds to Kernberg's concept of being able to differentiate self images from object images.

According to Kernberg, a failure in this developmental task—the ability to differentiate self images from object images, to test reality, and to separate intrapsychically from one's mother—is the core developmental defect in the psychotic individual. The borderline patient, basically, has been able to accomplish this developmental task; for him the main developmental problem comes later. Although the borderline individual has accomplished this task to a major extent compared to the psychotic, this mastery sometimes remains far from total. This explains the ease with which reality testing in the borderline patient can break down under stress or in close interpersonal relationships.

As noted, according to Kernberg, even before the child has accomplished the developmental task of self–object differentiation, from early infancy on, he organizes his experiences according to whether the experiences are perceived as positive or negative. By age 1½, when the child has developed object permanency (Piaget's [1954] concept of a stable visual representation of the mother whether she is present or absent), he still views others as either all-good or all-bad. This tendency to perceive objects as all-good or all-bad, earlier described by Klein (1946), is called splitting. It is not until the child is between the ages of 2 and 3 (usually closer to 3) that he stops using splitting as a primary organizing principle. In a gradual process described eloquently by McDevitt (1975), the child gives up splitting and attains libidinal object constancy.

The attainment of libidinal object constancy is the developmental task that is lacking in the borderline individual. Although Kernberg does not use the term *libidinal object constancy,* he states that the borderline patient has failed in the task of "the integration of self and object images built up under the influence of libidinal drive derivatives with the corresponding self and object images built up under the influence of aggressive drive derivatives" (1967, p. 664). This is equivalent to saying that the borderline individual has not attained libidinal object constancy and that he still uses splitting as a primary organizing principle.

The tendency of the borderline patient to utilize splitting is not an all-or-none phenomenon. Just as the psychotic does not always test reality poorly, the borderline does not always split. It is more that the borderline patient had some difficulty, varying from individual to individual, with completing the developmental task of attaining libidinal object constancy. Depending on the individual, this problem can show itself, at one extreme, as an ever-present defect in this area, or at the other extreme, as a defect that only occurs defensively under stress. Although Kernberg emphasizes the defensive nature of splitting, it seems reasonable to conclude that the majority of borderline patients will fall somewhere between these two extremes.

According to Kernberg, the difficulty in integrating good and bad self and object image (or positive and negative introjects) is the core problem in the borderline patient. It is the presence of an excessive amount of aggressive drive in the earliest (pregenital) years of life that is the basic etiologic factor. This aggressive drive interferes with the unfolding of the separation-individuation process in such a way that splitting is reinforced and libidinal object constancy is never truly attained. The excessive aggressive drive is thought to be due either to congenital factors or to be secondary to severe early frustrations. Regarding borderline psychopathology, this problem becomes of critical importance after the child has completed (or relatively completed) the developmental task of differentiating self and object images, and before he has attained libidinal object constancy. To be more specific, Kernberg (1980) feels that the critical developmental period for most borderline individuals coincides with the rapprochement subphase of the separation-individuation phase. However, in a small group of borderline patients, the critical period coincides with the differentiation subphase.

The borderline individual's inability to integrate good and bad self and object images leads to a multitude of consequences. There is a propensity toward splitting and to the use of other borderline defenses, such as primitive idealization, projection and projective identification, primitive denial, devaluation, and omnipotence. The use of these primitive defenses casts a negative influence on interpersonal relations and on the adaptation to reality. There is a propensity for primitive affect states and for affective instability, along with poor frustration tolerance and poor impulse control. The borderline patient's concept of himself and others is unintegrated and fragmentary. Meaningful comprehensive images of himself and others are elusive, and an unintegrated identity, or identity diffusion, is characteristic. The presence of all-good and all-bad images also leads to problems with superego integration. The ego ideal is often overidealized, based on all-good self and object images. The conscience often includes sadistic components based on all-bad images and is easily externalized. Depending on the degree with which the borderline individual has completed the developmental task of differentiating self and object images, there can also be a tendency for episodic problems in reality testing and conceptual thinking.

ADLER'S THEORETICAL MODEL

Although Adler agrees with Kernberg that borderline patients experience difficulty in integrating good and bad self images and object images, he believes that this problem arises at a later point in development and at a later time in treatment than is generally thought. He does not consider this difficulty the core problem in borderline patients. For Adler, the core difficulty is a functional insufficiency and instability of a certain kind of introject, which he calls the holding introject. It is the *lack* of this specific introject, rather than a difficulty in integrating contradictory introjects, that he considers crucial.

Adler's conceptual model for normal development is somewhat different, although not necessarily contradictory, from that of Kernberg. Clearly borrowing from the concepts of Winnicott (1953, 1965) and Kohut (1971, 1977, 1984), Adler believes that for the infant to achieve significant autonomy, two qualities of experience are essential. One is narcissistic, relating to feelings of personal value, and the other is holding and soothing. Adler hypothesizes that good-enough mothering is necessary in early life to provide these two essential experiences. Deficiencies with the narcissistic experience are ultimately related to both narcissistic and borderline patients. Deficiencies in the holding and soothing experience are more specifically related to borderline individuals.

The infant needs the mother initially as an external object or selfobject to provide holding and soothing. Adler uses the term *selfobject* to refer to a person who provides functions necessary to maintain a dependent individual's psychological integrity. The selfobject is experienced as part of the self by the individual. At around 8 months, the infant attains recognition memory (Fraiberg 1969), the capacity to recognize an object as familiar, even though he cannot yet evoke the memory of the object. Recognition memory makes possible the beginnings of an inner representational world. It is only from this point, and not before, that Adler speaks of self images and object images (or representations).

With the attainment of recognition memory, if there has been good-enough mothering, the child can begin to use transitional objects to provide the holding and soothing that were only provided previously by the physical presence of the mother. At around 18 months, the infant attains evocative memory (Fraiberg 1969), the capacity to remember an object without being reminded of its existence by external cues. With this attainment, the holding and soothing provided previously only by the mother as a selfobject, or by transitional objects, can be internalized as holding introjects. Adler believes that an introject must have the characteristic of being continually available for the individual. Thus, the development of evocative memory is a prerequisite for introject formation. As the holding introjects become enduring and stabilized, the child is in a position to give up both transitional objects and selfobjects for holding and soothing.

In borderline patients, good-enough mothering is

lacking in early life. Thus, the mother is not optimally available for necessary holding and soothing. This deficiency impairs the children's ability to use transitional objects for holding and soothing and to attain solid evocative memory. These individuals are unable to internalize holding introjects adequately; they remain dependent on external selfobjects to provide the needed holding and soothing.

The adult borderline patient, dependent on external objects (or selfobjects) for holding and soothing, is especially vulnerable to separation. Although he usually maintains his psychological integrity and avoids undue separation anxiety by sufficient interaction with holding selfobjects, he is exceptionally vulnerable to disruptions in these relationships. Disruptions ensue when the patient perceives the significant other as not performing the holding function to the degree needed. This often precipitates rage, which precipitates regression. Adler uses the term *aloneness* to describe a kind of inner emptiness and sometimes panic that characterizes a patient who needs a holding selfobject but who does not have one. When the borderline individual feels that he is in danger of losing his holding selfobjects, he uses a number of methods to try to maintain or regain these selfobjects. Under the sway of regression, fusion and incorporation are used to aid in this task. This, in itself, however, presents a threat of destruction of the self or the selfobject, and is a poor solution. Here the borderline individual is faced with the need-fear dilemma, of risking acute separation anxiety by losing the selfobject, or of risking destruction of the self and/or selfobject by attempting to retain the selfobject via fusion and incorporation.

COMPARISON AND INTEGRATION OF THE TWO MODELS

At first glance, Kernberg and Adler seem far apart in their theoretical understanding regarding borderline patients. They emphasize different phenomena, they construct different theoretical frameworks, and they use different terminology. By labeling Kernberg's theory an "ambivalence theory" and referring to his own as a theory of "insufficiency," Adler is emphasizing the differences. Waldinger (1987) takes this contrast a step further by juxtaposing Kernberg's "conflict" model and Adler's "deficit" model. Waldinger states that corresponding to their differences in theory, Kernberg considers interpretation the main psychotherapeutic intervention in borderline patients, whereas Adler places primary emphasis on experiential learning (within a holding environment).

Let us focus on the supposed contrast of conflict versus deficiency in Kernberg's and Adler's writings. Using the ego-psychological diagnostic approach, elaborated in Chapter 1, the borderline individual is described as having four relative ego strengths and four underlying ego weaknesses. The relative strengths include reality testing, thought processes, interpersonal relations, and adaptation to reality; whereas the underlying weaknesses include the combination of poor impulse control and poor frustration tolerance, the proclivity to use primitive ego defenses, identity diffusion, and affective instability. By the ego-psychological diagnostic approach, clearly compatible with Kernberg, the weaknesses can certainly qualify, at least partially, as deficits. Similarly, the core problem in the borderline patient, according to Kernberg, the difficulty in integrating good and bad self and object images with the corresponding lack of attainment of libidinal object constancy, can also be considered a partial deficit. I do not claim that Kernberg would agree with this; yet, one reading of his work, in accordance with the above, is that the borderline patient has relative deficits. Certainly there is much conflict, with the conflict centering on the areas of relative deficiency. Thus, regarding conflict versus deficiency, it is not either/or but both/and.

Correspondingly, although Adler classifies his theory as one of insufficiency, he does not omit the role of conflict. He hypothesizes a deficit in holding introjects, although this deficit itself need only be thought of as partial. However, as the borderline patient attempts to overcome this deficit by relating with holding selfobjects in the environment, conflict emerges. This conflict, which Adler describes in detail, involves rage, regression, various kinds of painful affects, anxiety, and defense. Again, the conflict centers upon the areas of deficiency. Thus, for Adler as for Kernberg, the conflict versus deficiency issue is not either/or but both/and.

Adler describes the emergence of conflict when he talks of psychotherapy. He emphasizes experiential learning within a holding environment, but never says that this learning goes on silently. In fact, he emphasizes the conflict that emerges when psychodynamic obstacles block the patient from using the therapist as a selfobject and from internalizing the holding function. In this context, interpretation and insight are necessary aspects of the psychotherapeutic work. Analogously, Kernberg's emphasis on interpretation does not mean that interpretative work does not occur in a holding environment. As elaborated in Chapter 8, psychotherapeutic approaches can be arranged on a continuum from most insight-oriented to most supportive. These approaches include psychoanalysis, analytically oriented psychotherapy, modified analytically oriented psychotherapy, dynamically oriented psychotherapy, and supportive psychotherapy. Within this model, both Adler and Kernberg utilize modified analytically oriented psychotherapy.

Let us now examine some similarities regarding Adler's and Kernberg's theories. Kernberg speaks of the emergence of discrete units of self images and object images at around 8 months. According to Adler, this is the same time that infants obtain recognition memory, making an inner representational world possible. Adler believes that at around 18 months, the normal infant attains evocative memory. Kernberg's concept of object permanency clearly corresponds to this time frame.

Adler believes that the absence of solid evocative memory by this time leads to the core deficiency in the borderline patient, the inadequate formation of holding introjects. Kernberg also believes that this period is when the borderline patient is most vulnerable, during the rapprochement subphase of the separation-individuation process. Adler emphasizes a lack of good-enough mothering at this time as an essential element. Kernberg, in addition to congenital factors, certainly allows for this possibility in hypothesizing early frustration as a definite factor in leading to excessive aggression. Analogously, Adler speaks of rage by the borderline patient in response to frustrations of the selfobjects. Although Adler and Kernberg emphasize different phenomena and use different terminology, what they say is not incompatible. In fact, the main incompatibility may be the relative failure for each to address the phenomenon that the other emphasizes.

In a simplified manner, it is possible to combine Adler's and Kernberg's seemingly differing theories into one integrated model. A primary problem in the early life of the borderline individual is the lack of good-enough mothering and/or the child's relative inability to perceive the mothering as good enough. This latter possibility can be influenced by congenital factors. This "lack" of mothering contributes to early frustration and to the upsurge of aggressive drive, and it interferes with the unfolding of the separation-individuation process and with the development of introjective configurations. All these difficulties peak at the rapprochement subphase of the separation-individuation process, thus disrupting the establishment of solid evocative memory and object permanency and resulting in insufficient internalization of positive (holding) introjects. Positive (holding) introjects are both quantitatively inadequate and unstable, and when formed, are kept away from the negative introjects. Thus, there is difficulty in the integration of positive and negative introjects. Again, the problem is both/and, not either/or. Both the deficiency in holding introjects and the difficulty in integrating positive and negative introjects are core problems for the borderline individual.

One of Kernberg's premises is that the infant normally organizes his experiences according to good and bad affect states. Research (Lichtenberg 1983, Stern 1985) casts some questions on this aspect of Kernberg's theory. There are questions whether this phenomenon occurs normally as opposed to pathologically, as well as questions regarding the timing of this phenomenon. With this in mind, this aspect of Kernberg's theory has been omitted from the integrated model. It might be noted, however, that this phenomenon is theoretically compatible with the integrated approach.

ETIOLOGY

This is a good place to comment on etiology. Deprivation, privation, and neglect have been implicated as etiological in some borderline patients. In others, a pattern of overindulgent, overintrusive, and overstimulating mothering has been noted. Here the primary caretaker forms an engulfing, suffocating, and fused relationship with the borderline-to-be child, not allowing him to separate and individuate and to become autonomous (Masterson 1976, 1978, Rinsley 1978, 1982). Additionally, there is a growing literature showing a high percentage of borderline individuals with a history of trauma, of physical and/or sexual abuse (Herman et al. 1989, Ogata et al. 1990, Stone 1990a, Zanarini et al. 1989). Neglect, overindulgence, and trauma all can play an etiologic role, but in different borderline patients.

Kernberg and Adler, in their developmental theories, talk about the internal structure of the borderline child, its development and sequelae. They do not specify what happens in the external world to cause the problems in internal structure. Although Kernberg hypothesizes too much aggression as etiologic, he does not say what causes this overabundance of aggression. It could be innate, or it could be environmental. Trauma, neglect, or overindulgence could all play a role. Likewise, Adler suggests that there are failures in the early mothering without specifying what the failures are. Again, the failures could be those of trauma, neglect, or overindulgence. The theories of Kernberg and Adler are not reviewed because they provide etiological answers. Rather, they provide excellent theoretical frameworks for both understanding and doing psychotherapy with borderline individuals.

CLINICAL EXAMPLES

Clinically, borderline patients exhibit deficits in positive holding introjects, as well as difficulties in integrating good and bad self images and object images. Some patients primarily demonstrate the former, while others primarily demonstrate the latter. Still other borderline patients show both problems simultaneously, at least to some extent, even early in treatment. Thus some patients conform to Adler's theory; others, to Kernberg's theory; and still others, to both. Virtually all borderline patients, however, reflect the parameters of the integrated approach, which is clinically useful because of its broad applicability.

Many borderline patients rapidly reveal one or both core problems in the treatment setting, most obviously in the transference. Sometimes these problems arise with an intensity and within the context of resistance that demands immediate psychotherapeutic intervention. I will cite several typical clinical examples of patients who would clearly be diagnosed as borderline.

Ms. G

From the beginning of her psychotherapy sessions, this patient had marked difficulty viewing her therapist positively. She perceived him as lacking and deficient, and much of what he did or said confirmed this view in her mind. Whenever she was uncertain, Ms. G imposed a negative interpretation on the therapist's words and actions. Thus, she objected to the therapist's fee policy, found it insulting that he did not have an ashtray next to her seat, and felt it was intolerable if he fidgeted in his chair. For Ms. G to see the therapist as having any worth, he had to demonstrate his empathy, his thoughtfulness, and his insight clearly. After sessions in which the therapist did, in fact, demonstrate his worth, Ms. G would feel good about him, at least for several days. Then in his absence, she would begin again to view him as flawed. Because of this, she was often reluctant to come to her next appointment. Months and months were devoted to exploring the patient's feelings toward her therapist, and to connecting those feelings to her childhood, when her mother and father both had regularly devalued and made fun of her. Ms. G had had tremendous difficulty internalizing her parents as positive holding introject. Thus, although the patient could possibly be viewed as using splitting (in that she usually saw her therapist as basically bad but sometimes good), the primary problem here appears to be the lack of stable internalized holding introjects.

Mr. K

On admission to a hospital unit, Mr. K developed an immediate idealized transference to his female therapist. He viewed her as the best therapist in the hospital, if not the country. She was omnipotent and omniscient, clearly the perfect therapist for him. In contrast, Mr. K viewed many of the other hospital personnel on his treatment team as insensitive, stupid, and worthless. Unfortunately, the therapist was a beginner and unfamiliar with treating borderline patients. She was gratified by her patient's adulation and never commented on the defensive nature of this behavior. When Mr. K was discharged 6 weeks after admission, she offered him several early morning outpatient appointment times. These times did not optimally suit Mr. K, and he tried to persuade his therapist to change them by 15 minutes. When she could not, Mr. K rapidly concluded that his once near-perfect therapist was not worth anything anyway, so he refused follow-up outpatient treatment. The problem clearly was Mr. K's difficulty in integrating good and bad object images. He was able to rapidly establish a positive, although primitive, all-good image of his therapist, but under frustration, the image rapidly reverted to all-bad. Not unexpectedly, after his frustration with the therapist, Mr. K suddenly began to view other members of his treatment teams more positively.

Mr. T

This patient entered psychotherapy displaying a clear neediness and clingingness to his therapist. Unfortunately, he also exhibited a lack of commitment and trust. He gave his therapist the benefit of the doubt and spoke openly and fluently, yet was always scrutinizing the therapist to see if he was in fact trustworthy. If Mr. T perceived his therapist as lacking in any way, he would rapidly come to see him as a totally bad person, insensitive, insincere, self-centered, and interested only in money. Sometimes Mr. T would even view the therapist as evil and potentially harmful to him. The patient viewed the therapist in this all-bad way early in the treatment, when he changed Mr. T's therapy appointment, when he took a week off, and when he once appeared to be daydreaming. At those times, Mr. T was strongly tempted to discontinue therapy, but the therapist provided clear-cut reality testing, enabling Mr. T to remain in treatment. The therapist told Mr. T directly that he was not as bad as Mr. T thought. Rather, Mr. T was sensitive to feeling hurt and belittled by rejections or lapses that the therapist might have made inadvertently. In contrast, at other times early in the treatment process, when Mr. T found the therapist empathic, he viewed him as all-good, wonderful, even godlike.

Thus, the patient's feelings about his therapist fluctuated widely from all-good to all-bad, but always with an underlying lack of trust. Many months passed before Mr. T began to perceive his therapist more consistently and trustingly. Mr. T, although suffering from the lack of stable internalized holding introjects, also clearly demonstrated his difficulty in integrating good and bad object images. Mr. T thus appears to be a borderline patient who demonstrated both core problems early in the treatment situation.

4

PROGNOSIS AND REFERRAL YIELD

PROGNOSIS

Turning to prognosis, the studies of McGlashan (1985, 1986) and Stone (1990a) provide important and similar findings. Stone's book, describing the long-term follow-up study of 502 hospitalized patients, will be discussed here (Goldstein 1992). The findings of this study certainly create an optimistic attitude regarding prognosis.

To get to the bottom line first, the borderline patients in the study, given time, tended to get better. In fact, two out of three of these patients got better; this was in marked contrast to the group of schizophrenic patients, in which approximately one out of ten improved. Only one of four borderline patients required rehospitalization, as compared to three out of four in the schizophrenic group. Most borderline patients went back to school, managed a household, held a job, or pursued a career over 50 percent of the time since leaving the hospital.

Despite this overall positive picture, outcomes varied

considerably, in accordance with a variety of factors. The best outcome was associated with patients having artistic talent, an obsessive-compulsive personality style, a very high IQ, and/or general attractiveness. The general characteristics of likableness, candor, perseverance, and talent were also associated with good outcome. Alcoholism, where there was definitive treatment in Alcoholics Anonymous, also provided a good prognosis. Bad outcome was associated with patients who had served time in jail, had committed rape, and who had an antisocial personality. Males who eloped, women who were subjected to incest by their fathers, and patients suffering brutality in childhood had negative outcomes. Borderline patients characterized by six of the *DSM-III* items also did poorly.

A typical pattern for the majority of the borderline patients was to remain dysfunctional for a few years after hospitalization. As the patients entered their thirties, they began to improve. This was possibly related to a developmental "mellowing" and/or to results of treatment. Most patients continued to improve into their forties, often with the loss of "tempestuous qualities." However, many patients remained vulnerable to regression, such that unanticipated stress and losses in mid-life would easily reawaken old symptoms.

The relationship of psychotherapy to improvement was difficult to evaluate. An impression was that insight-oriented psychotherapy was helpful to a select group of the borderline patients. Those best suited for this endeavor were people of high motivation, good psychological-mindedness, a low degree of early trauma, and only a minimum of impulsivity.

Regarding background, 50 percent of the borderline women had a history of incest, as compared to 5 percent of women in general. According to Dr. Stone, incest and its psychological sequelae appeared to play a definitive role in these patients in the pathogenesis of the borderline syndrome. Incest was most pathogenic when it was transgenerational, involved force, was chronic, and occurred within the span of the victim's memory. Dr. Stone hypothesized that the increased incidence of the borderline diagnosis in women as opposed to men (145 vs. 61 in this study) could be attributed to this etiological factor. Parental brutality also was very common in the histories of borderline patients. The combination of transgenerational incest plus parental brutality was seen to be devastating. Regarding the same study, incest and brutality loomed as important predisposing factors as compared to separation and loss. The latter, Dr. Stone hypothesized, might play a larger role in outpatient samples.

Regarding suicide, the overall rate among the borderline sample was 9 percent. In borderline patients with concomitant major affective disorder, the rate went up to 18 percent. The highest suicide rate was in borderline patients with both major affective disorder and alcohol or drug abuse. A sense of hopelessness and a proneness to violence provided a lethal combination regarding suicide.

REFERRAL YIELD

I will take a moment at this point to introduce the concept of referral yield. By referral yield I mean the percentage of patients referred for therapy who actually continue for a reasonable period of time. In my experience, with neurotic patients, when referred in a positive (as opposed to a neutral) manner, this approaches 100 percent. By contrast, with borderline patients, this is exceptionally low. The borderline patient looks for the ideal: the therapist with whom he feels comfortable; the one with whom he feels the right vibrations, the right wavelength, the right sensations; the therapist who he feels is similar to himself, who has the same values, philosophy, and upbringing; the therapist whom he feels at one with, secure, happy, and content. Often the patient insists on interviewing multiple therapists, until finally one meets his fantasized needs.

Possibly sensing his own vulnerability to the selfobject relationship that he will eventually form, he looks for a therapist with whom he is optimally comfortable. He very much needs a therapist who is stable, competent, consistent, and secure; yet he often chooses his therapist by what he intuitively feels during one interview, relying on his all-or-none feelings of the moment.

5

PROJECTIVE IDENTIFICATION

Dr. A came out of a psychotherapy session feeling inadequate about himself and pessimistic about his work with his patient, Ms. B. He briefly wondered if Ms. B might be better off with a different therapist. Dr. A was quite puzzled about having these feelings and thoughts. He had always believed that he did good work in general and with Ms. B in particular. He took a look at himself and concluded that he was generally an optimistic young man, usually viewing himself as competent and quite adequate. So where did these feelings come from?

It is a rather common occurrence for psychotherapists to leave therapy sessions experiencing some unwanted and uncomfortable feelings. They might, for instance, feel anxious, depressed, overwhelmed, or even confused. Like Dr. A, they might feel inadequate or overly pessimistic. Sometimes they are puzzled by their feelings, unclear why they feel the way they do. In situations like this, a therapist has learned to look at the countertransference—to ask himself or herself, "Is there something within me, based on my past, that has stimulated such a feeling? Am I prone to feeling anxious, am I vulnerable to depression, do I easily feel inadequate?" Sometimes the answer does lie in the countertransference, at least partially. Often, however, it lies mainly elsewhere.

What is often happening in instances like these is that the therapists have come under the influence of projective identifications. They are feeling uncomfortable not so much because of their own unresolved conflicts (although these should always be considered and never easily discounted), but because the patients have projected these feelings onto them. In fact, not only have the patients projected their feelings onto the therapists, they have done everything in their power to make the therapists accept the projections. They have interacted with the therapists, sometimes overtly, sometimes more subtly, to get them to think, act, and feel in accordance with the projections. Sometimes feeling coerced and pressured, therapists have accepted the projections, frequently not realizing what has taken place. They have responded to the projective identifications, not so much because of their conflicts as related to their countertransference, but because of the pressure from the patients for them to receive the projections.

Going back to the example, when Dr. A looked closely at the psychotherapy hour, he could see how Ms. B, suffering from chronic feelings of inadequacy and low self-esteem, had projected these feelings onto him, then acted toward him so that he would accept the projected feelings. Ms. B succeeded in her task, and by the end of the hour Dr. A felt inadequate himself. Ms. B was subtle enough in her interactions with Dr. A so that he was initially puzzled by his feelings.

During the psychotherapy hour, Ms. B first spoke of how worthless she was and how hopeless her condition was. Then she discussed psychotherapy in general, wondering how useful it was in serious cases. She then went on to discuss a series of cases where an inexperienced professional had erred. A young lawyer had made a major mistake that lost him a large amount of money, an inexperienced surgeon had left his patient with an unsightly scar, and a new accountant had totally messed up Ms. B's taxes. Experience was all-important, Ms. B claimed, and asked if Dr. A didn't think so. Ms. B then began to argue her point with Dr. A, insisting that he agree with her. She then recalled a number of stupid blunders Dr. A had made, but said it was "no big deal" because she realized he had just completed his psychiatric training. She viewed her case as a very serious one, yet she knew Dr. A would try as hard as he could. However, she felt she had suffered for so long that possibly no one could help her.

This example shows projective identification in the psychotherapy hour, but this process is not confined to psychotherapy. It is a commonplace phenomenon in day-to-day interactions between friends and acquaintances, as some of the later examples will demonstrate.

As presented in the example of Dr. A and Ms. B, projective identification appears to be a fairly straightforward phenomenon. Yet, because the term is currently used in numerous different ways by many different people, it remains a most elusive and difficult concept. It has been described as a primitive defense in patients with borderline and psychotic disorders, a developmental process out of which self and object differentiation comes about, an integral part of the transference–countertransference process in both psychoanalysis and psychotherapy, a form of empathy, and more. Clinically, some view projective identification as a useful and even necessary way of conceptualizing a variety of phenomena, some use the term sparingly but with clear meaning, and others have little use for the concept. For those who use the term, there are many questions. These include the difference between projective identification and projection, the nature of the identification and how it relates to the projection, the role of blurring of ego boundaries in the process, the role of the interaction between the projector and the recipient of the projection, and the nature of the reinternalization process.

Melanie Klein (1946) first described projective identification as a process beginning in the earliest time of life, in a phase she called the paranoid-schizoid position. Klein was referring to a process in which parts of the self are split off and projected into another person, leading to a particular kind of identification. This process includes an effort to control the other person by the projected parts. Segal (1964) summarized Klein's original description of projective identification in a more succinct manner: "Parts of the self and internal objects are split off and projected into the external object, which then becomes possessed by, controlled and identified with the projected parts" (p. 27). The concept of projective identification has been developed and elaborated by many of Klein's followers, including Bion (1959a,b), Rosenfeld (1952, 1954), and Segal (1964). More recent contributions along these lines have been made by Malin and Grotstein (1966), Grotstein (1981), and Ogden (1979, 1982, 1986).

Although always an important concept in the Kleinian school of psychoanalysis, the term *projective identification* attained increasing popularity and became more generally widespread with the publication of Kernberg's work on the borderline personality organization (1967). Kernberg listed projective identification as one of the borderline defenses, together with splitting, primitive idealization, primitive denial, omnipotence, and devaluation. As detailed later in this chapter, Kernberg's thinking about projective identification has evolved with time, and his original description of the term is somewhat different from his more recent elaborations (1987a,b). The increased use of the term, unfortunately, has not led to a consensus as to its meaning. In fact, there have been new applications of the concept and new ways of looking at projective identification. Examples include the use of the concept by the object-relations-oriented family therapists (Shapiro et al. 1977, Zinner 1976; Zinner and Shapiro 1972) and Porder's innovative and useful thinking about projective identification (1987).

The history of the concept of projective identification has

been elaborated quite well by others (Grotstein 1981, Meissner 1980, Sandler 1987) and will not be repeated here. Rather, in this chapter I focus on the various current usages of the term, with the hope of providing added clarification and integration. The emphasis of this chapter is on projective identification as a defense mechanism, especially as it relates to the psychoanalytic and psychotherapeutic processes.

In this chapter, explanations of the various aspects and steps of projective identification are illustrated by clinical examples. Six detailed clinical examples appear at the end of the text, and excerpts from these cases will be interspersed throughout the chapter at appropriate places. At times, it might be useful for the reader to refer to the detailed clinical example after reading an excerpt.

REFERENCE MODEL OF PROJECTIVE IDENTIFICATION

To look at the different current usages of projective identification, I use a broad model of projective identification as a point of reference. This broad model is in accordance with the work of Ogden (1979, 1982), who originally defined projective identification as a process occurring in three steps. Step 1 involves the fantasy of projecting a part of oneself into another person, with that part controlling the person from within. The projected part is something the individual wishes to be rid of, either because the part threatens to destroy the self from within or because the person feels the part is in danger of attack by other aspects of the self. A distinction is made here between projective identification and projection. In projective identification, the projector feels at one with the recipient of the projection; this feeling of oneness involves a blurring of self and object representations. In contrast, in projection proper, the projector feels estranged from and threatened by the recipient of the projection.

Step 2 is an interpersonal interaction in which the projector actively pressures the recipient to think, feel, and act in accordance with the projection. According to Ogden, projective identification does not exist when there is no interaction of this nature.

Finally, in step 3, the projection is reinternalized after it has been psychologically possessed by the recipient. The nature of the reinternalization process depends on the maturational level of the projector and can range from primitive types of introjection to mature forms of identification. Whatever the process, the reinternalization offers the projector the potential for attaining new ways of handling a set of feelings and fantasies that he or she could only wish to be rid of in the past.

More recently, Ogden (1986) has clarified that the projection can involve either a self representation or an object representation. He has de-emphasized the concept of controlling the person from within and has backed away from the need for a blurring of self and object representations as necessary to the process. With these recent clarifications, Ogden's concept of projective identification now provides the broadest model today.

Some (Kernberg 1987a,b, Sandler 1987) feel that Ogden's concept of projective identification is too broad. However, it is just that aspect of his work that makes it conducive as a reference to compare the various current usages of projective identification. In using his work as a reference, I will modify and outline Ogden's steps in the following fashion: Step 1 is the projection (or externalization) of part of oneself onto an external object (recipient). Step 1a is the blurring of self and object representations. Step 2 is the interpersonal interaction in which the projector actively pressures the recipient to think, feel, and act in accordance with the projection. Step 3 is the reinternalization of the projection after the projection has been psychologically processed (and modified) by the recipient.

As will be shown in this chapter, the different definitions of projective identification relate to exactly how one conceptualizes the term *projection* in step 1, whether step 1-a is deemed necessary, and how many of the three steps are required for the process to qualify as projective identification.

STEP 1: THE PROJECTION

What is meant by the term *projection* is very important because people who use the term *projective identification* differ in their definition of projection. Sandler (1987) defines projection as involving a transfer of mental content from a self representation to an object representation. Meissner (1980) is basically in agreement with this, stating that projection involves an attribution of part of a self representation to an object representation. Meissner further distinguishes displacement from projection, stating that displacement involves an attribution of part of one object representation to another object representation. Differentiation of projection from displacement in this way is often the norm. Yet Ogden (1979, 1982) classifies displacement (of one object representation to another) as a form of projection. The question of the definition of projection is crucial here. As will be seen, the process of projective identification takes on different meanings in accordance with what part of the psychic apparatus is projected.

For further clarification, I first simplistically state the obvious, that the psychic apparatus is thought to include the drives (id), the ego, and the superego. Next I state that I view self and object representations as parts of the ego (Goldstein 1985). Although this is in accordance with the ideas of Sandler and Rosenblatt (1960), Jacobson (1964), and Kernberg (1976), some (Boesky 1983) disagree. Some prefer to think of self and object representations as being formed by the interaction of ego, id, and superego; additionally, some object to combining the representational model with structural theory. However, including self and object representations as parts of the ego allows for an easily understandable model, clearly suitable for the purposes of this chapter.

Next, again in accordance with the purposes of this chapter, I simplify things and use the term *projection* in its broadest sense to include any kind of externalization. Although the term *externalization* is sometimes differentiated from the term *projection,* often referring to a larger group of phenomena, it is also widely used as a synonym for projection (Sandler 1987). This latter usage will be applied here. Thus, we can speak of externalizations or projections as referring to drives, self representations, object representations, and superego. Alternatively, one can think totally in accordance with a representational model. Here drives would be conceptualized as self representations (either aggressive self representations or libidinal self representations), and the superego would be conceptualized as an object representation.

Given these simplifications, I now posit a number of distinctions and ideas regarding step 1 of projective identification. I want to emphasize that these ideas need to be viewed as generalizations only, as ideas that warrant further exploration and thinking.

The nature of projective identification changes in accordance with what is projected. A very important distinction here is between the projection of self representations or drives, on the one hand, and the projection of object representations or superego, on the other. In general, the projection of self representations (or drives) is thought to constitute a more primitive process than the projection of object representations (or superego). Projections of self representations (or drives), when they occur frequently, are most typical of individuals with borderline and psychotic disorders. Regarding the psychotherapeutic process, these types of projections may occur in neurotic individuals, especially in the transference regression in psychoanalysis; however, with neurotic individuals, they are neither frequent nor predominant. In contrast, in psychotherapy with patients with borderline and psychotic disorders, these kinds of projections can be both frequent and predominant, even without the use of the couch.

The projection of object representations (or superego) constitutes a different phenomenon. Traditionally, when one thinks of the transference as a repetition of actual relations from the past, fantasized relations from the past, and defenses against both, one is referring to projections of object representations. Projections of object representations (or superego) are ubiquitous; they are commonplace among all individuals, both in day-to-day interactions and within psychotherapy. As noted, projections of object representations are synonymous with displacements. To help illustrate the different types of projection in step 1, I refer now to the clinical examples.

In case 1, Mr. C views his analyst as treating him unfairly and taking advantage of him. This view of his analyst is heightened when Mr. C anticipates that the analyst will charge for a missed session. Mr. C has a long history of feeling taken advantage of and used by his mother. This case is an example of a transference based on the projection of an object representation.

In case 2, Ms. D presents herself as inadequate, little, and pathetic, and then feels that her analyst views her in that same way. Actually, her analyst views her as competent and high-powered, yet she insists that he sees her as little and inadequate. Here Ms. D is experiencing with her analyst what she continually experienced with her father as a child. This is another, more complicated, example of a transference based on the projection of an object representation. Here Ms. D retains her self representation (little and inadequate) and projects onto the analyst an object representation of someone who treats her in accordance with that self representation.

In case 4, Mr. G views his therapist as worthless and impotent, incapable of doing anything right. In reality, the therapist is doing an excellent job. Mr. G, having grown up in an environment where he was continually attacked and belittled by his mother, has internalized an image of himself as worthless and impotent. This case is an example of a transference based on the projection of a self representation of someone worthless and impotent.

In case 5, Mr. H does things to make his girlfriend feel anxious. For example, when in a crisis he leaves out crucial details, which makes the situation seem more dangerous. Then he complains bitterly of his girlfriend's high anxiety. Actually, Mr. H is the one who is overtly anxious, and he deals with his anxiety by projecting it onto his girlfriend. This is an example of the projection of a self representation of someone who is anxious.

If only projections of self representations (and drives) are included in the definition of projective identification, it refers mostly to a process involving individuals with borderline and psychotic disorders. This process, often thought to include some blurring of ego boundaries, is basically in accordance with the thinking of Kernberg (1987a,b) and Meissner (1980). If projections of object representations (and superego) are included in the definition of projective identification, and if blurring of ego boundaries is not required, then projective identification refers to a process involving basically all individuals. This is in accordance with the work of Grotstein (1981) and with Ogden's more recent use of the term (1986). Both Ogden and Grotstein basically view projective identification as a universal feature of the transference. Interesting enough, in the case examples just cited, Mr. C and Ms. D are basically neurotic individuals, whereas Mr. G and Mr. H are psychotic.

At this point, I take the opportunity to relate the considerations just discussed to Meissner's concept of transference (1988) and to Racker's concept of countertransference (1957, 1968). Meissner divides transferences into two groups: projection transferences and displacement transferences. Projection transferences involve projections of self representations, whereas displacement transferences involve projections of object representations. For Meissner, in accordance with what I have already stated, projection transferences are most typical of individuals with borderline and psychotic disorders, whereas displacement transferences are more typical of neurotic individuals. Meissner would view the transferences involving Mr. C and Ms. D, where there are projections of object representations, as displacement transferences. He would view Mr. G as an example of a projection transference. Mr. H would be viewed as a projection transference, but outside of the psychotherapeutic situation.

Meissner's concept of transference corresponds to Racker's concept of countertransference (1957, 1968). Racker divides countertransference identifications into two types: concordant identifications, where the analyst identifies with the patient's internal structure (or self representations), and complementary identifications, where the analyst identifies with the patient's internal objects (or object representations). The concordant identification corresponds to Meissner's projection transference, and the complementary identification corresponds to Meissner's displacement transference.

STEP 1-A: THE BLURRING OF SELF AND OBJECT REPRESENTATIONS

It is interesting that both Kernberg (1967, 1975) and Ogden (1979, 1982) originally emphasized the blurring of self and object representations as part of projective identification, but then moved away from including it in the definition. In more recent descriptions of projective identification by Kernberg (1987a,b) and Ogden (1986), the blurring of self and object representations has been conspicuously omitted, although neither author states the reasons for the omission.

In his original concept of projective identification, Kernberg (1967) stated that it was the lack of ego boundaries *per se* that led to the identification that followed the projection. The beauty of Kernberg's original concept, in applying it to patients with borderline disorders, is that these patients often exhibit blurring of ego boundaries in close interpersonal relationships, enabling projections in that context to take on the characteristics of projective identification. As stated, in more recent writings, Kernberg (1987a,b) has removed step 1a from his definition of projective identification. Although in his view projective identification is a more primitive defense than projection itself, it is no longer considered an exclusively psychotic mechanism. However, in Kernberg's view, projective identification continues to be typical of individuals with borderline and psychotic disorders, and not typical of neurotic individuals.

Like Kernberg, Ogden (1979) originally emphasized that in protective identification, "the person involved in such a process is operating at least in part at a developmental level wherein there is profound blurring of boundaries between self and object representations" (p. 352). However, in his more recent book (1986), Ogden omits this blurring of ego boundaries when he described projective identification. Certainly, in viewing projective identification as a universal feature of the transference, Ogden no longer thinks in terms of blurring of self and object representations.

In accordance with the discussion of step 1, the blurring of ego boundaries in projective identification might be related to the nature of the projection. Projections of object representations (or superego) basically do not include the blurring of ego boundaries. However, projections of self representations (or drives) frequently include such a blurring. When one thinks about it, the transfer of a self representation to an object representation implies blurring of self and object representations by definition. The question remains whether projective identification is basically a psychotic process. Kernberg and Ogden were originally of that opinion, and Meissner (1980) still is. However, to the extent that the term has been broadened to include projections of object representations (and superego), it has become less exclusively associated with borderline conditions and psychoses.

Illustrations of the blurring of self and object representations occur most clearly in cases 5 and 6, involving a man with a borderline disorder and a psychotic man, respectively. In case 5, Mr. H does things to make his girlfriend feel anxious, then complains of her high anxiety level. There is a blurring of an anxious self representation with an anxious object representation. In case 6, Mr. I acts toward his therapist in a very disorganized and disruptive manner. He projects his disorganization onto his therapist but remains totally confused about whether he or she is disorganized. Here there is a blurring of a disorganized self representation with a disorganized object representation.

STEP 2: THE INTERPERSONAL INTERACTION

In this step, pressure is exerted by the projector on the recipient of the projection to think, feel, and act in accordance with the projection. Although some limit their concept of projective identification to step 1 and 1a only, most feel that step 2 is crucial in the projective identification process. Ogden (1979) states that "projective identification does not exist where there is no interaction between projector and object" (p. 359). Step 2 actually expands the concept of projective identification beyond the intrapsychic into the realm of interpersonal. In that regard, Ogden (1979, 1982) views projective identification as a bridging concept, one that links phenomena in the intrapsychic sphere with those in the interpersonal.

As noted, not everyone is happy with this expansion. In this regard, Meissner (1980) differentiates between the one-body context (intrapsychic) and the two-or-more body context (interpersonal). Meissner regards projective identification as a totally intrapsychic phenomenon and limits his concept to steps 1 and 1a. Kernberg (1987a) minimizes Meissner's differentiation, stating that it is artificial to separate the intrapsychic from the interpersonal. Despite this, Kernberg's original definition of projective identification (1967) is basically an intrapsychic one, whereas his more recent definition (1987a,b) clearly includes an interpersonal component.

Sandler (1987) helps us understand the various usages of projective identification by classifying projective identification into three stages, in accordance with the historical usages of the term. In stage 1, in accordance with Meissner, the processes remain intrapsychic. In stage 2, the analyst becomes involved in the interaction (step 2) by identifying with the projection to a degree sufficient to contribute to the analyst's countertransference. Here, the analyst is influenced by the projection only by his or her identification; the patient does not actively pressure the analyst to receive the projection. It is only in stage 3 that there is a definite interaction, where the analyst is pressured to act in accordance with the projection. In this stage, the opportunity for reinternalization, to be discussed later in this chapter, becomes available.

Illustrations of the interpersonal interaction, where pressure is exerted by the projector on the recipient to act in accordance with the projection, appear in all the clinical examples. In case 2, for example, Ms. D presents herself as inadequate, ineffective, little, and pathetic, and insists that her analyst view her this same way. She assumes that he agrees with her and presents one example after another based on this assumption. If the analyst states disagreement, she argues vehemently with him. With her persistence, the analyst feels pressured, coerced, overwhelmed, and frustrated.

Case 3 shows the interaction between two physicians during medical rounds. Here Dr. E, who is leading the rounds, projects her own feelings of inadequacy onto Dr. F and then treats Dr. F as if she is, in fact, inadequate, although Dr. F is almost her equal. As a result, Dr. F begins to feel inadequate herself.

In case 5, Mr. H projects his own anxiety onto his girlfriend. He talks to her about crisis situations, making the situations seem much more dangerous than they actually are. He then complains about her high anxiety.

In 1987, Porder presented projective identification in a different and interesting way. His work is mentioned now because it lends more understanding to the interpersonal interaction (step 2). Porder views projective identification as a "two-tiered" transference–countertransference mechanism, understood as a compromise formation that includes as major components identification with the aggressor and/or a turning of passive into active.

To understand Porder's work, I will use his example where, by means of projection in step 1, the analyst is viewed as a powerful aggressive parent, while the patient views himself or herself as a helpless victimized child. In step 2 (the interactive process), the patient becomes active and aggressive in trying to pressure the analyst to accept the projected image of a powerful aggressive parent. As the patient aggressively and forcefully tries to coerce the analyst to accept the projection, the analyst begins to feel helpless and victimized. Through this interpersonal interaction, a role reversal has taken place. The patient has identified with the powerful aggressive parent, turned passive into active, and is now treating the analyst as a helpless victim.

To clarify further, in step 1 the patient projects onto the analyst an object representation of a powerful parent, while identifying with a self representation of a helpless victimized child. Then in step 2, the patient projects onto the analyst a self representation of a victimized child, while identifying with an object representation of a powerful parent. Step 2, in this example, includes a second and different projection and a second and different identification. It should be noted that this is not always the case. For example, if in step 1 a self representation of a little, victimized self is projected, then step 2 simply adds intensity to the original projective process. However, step 2 always involves identification with the aggressor and a turning of passive into active.

Porder states that the interpersonal interactions characteristic of projective identification are more common in individuals with borderline and psychotic disorders. He relates this to the fact that these sicker individuals grow up with more disturbed and aggressive parents (by whom they are victimized and with whom they identify) and to the fact that these individuals have more difficulty expressing their conflicts verbally.

STEP 3: THE REINTERNALIZATION OF THE PROJECTION

In step 3, the projection is reinternalized after it has been psychologically processed and altered by the recipient. The psychological processing is in accordance with the recipient's psychic structure, including his or her strengths, weaknesses, and defensive system. If the recipient is sufficiently different from the projector, the processed version of the original projection might include substantial change. According to Ogden (1979, 1982), the processed version might be modified in such a way that the projector, after the reinternalization, might no longer feel the need to be rid of the now altered projection. Regarding psychotherapy, although the processing of the projection is often thought to take place "silently," interpretations regarding the projection can also be used to influence the reinternalization. The exact nature of the reinternalization process depends on the maturational level of the projector and can vary from primitive types of introjection to more mature forms of identification.

Step 3 extends the concept of projective identification even further. This step has particular relevance to the psychotherapeutic process. The reinternalization process offers the projector the potential for change, for attaining new ways of handling a set of feelings and fantasies that he or she could only wish to be rid of in the past. With that in mind, some (Grotstein 1981) have understood the essence of psychotherapeutic change as taking place through a series of projective identifications. The developmental process can be conceptualized in an analogous way.

As might be expected, the expansion of projective identification to step 3 is certainly not uniformly agreed upon. As noted, Meissner (1980) confines his definition of projective identification solely to an intrapsychic process, including steps 1 and 1a only. Kernberg (1987a,b), although he includes step 2 in his definition of projective identification, feels that step 3 would extend the definition too far. Sandler (1987) includes the reinternalization process only in what he calls stage 3 of projective identification. Despite these differences, the reinternalization process is now commonly included by many in thinking about projective identification.

Regarding the reinternalization process in psychotherapy, change usually can be noted only after the accumulation of a number of instances of reinternalization of projections. Case 2 demonstrates this. Ms. D presents herself as little and inadequate, repetitively insists that her analyst view her that way, and repetitively argues that, in fact, she is that way. As this process occurs over and over again, the analyst is partially influenced by what Ms. D says (that is, by her projections onto him); yet his basic view of her as competent and high-powered remains. With time, Ms. D is able to somewhat alter her self representation because of the reinternalization process. To be more specific, Ms. D repetitively projects onto the analyst an object representation of someone who views her in accordance with her self representation. The analyst is able to receive Ms. D's projections but is minimally influenced by them; he maintains his basic view of her as competent and high-powered. One could say that he modifies the projections onto him in accordance with his original view. By accumulative reinternalizations of the modified projections, Ms. D is gradually able to alter her self representation in accordance with the way the analyst views her. Thus, she is gradually able to see herself as less little and pathetic, and more competent and high-powered.

THE WORK OF ZINNER AND ASSOCIATES

As noted earlier, the concept of projective identification has been expanded to marital and family therapy by a group of object-relations-oriented psychoanalysts. The work of this group—Zinner, R. Shapiro, E. Shapiro, and Berkowitz (Shapiro et al. 1977; Zinner 1976; Zinner and Shapiro 1972)—is briefly reviewed here and related to the reference model of projective identification.

Regarding marriage, Zinner and colleagues emphasize mutual projective identifications between the marital couple, where each member willingly (although unconsciously) accepts the projections of the other. For example, a husband maintains a desired image of himself as aggressive and competitive by projecting his unwanted passive and helpless qualities onto his wife. This is ideal for the wife, who is able to maintain her desired image of a passive and helpless woman by projecting her competitive and aggressive qualities onto the husband. Thus, the projective identifications are mutually rewarding and complementary. In the case of parents and their children, projective identifications also can be complementary. More frequently, however, the child, although accepting of the parental projective identifications, suffers considerably as a result of the projections. Still, these children, for a variety of reasons, most important of which might be the fear of object loss, easily accept the parental projections.

In the work of Zinner and co-workers, it is noteworthy that the projections are typically easily accepted. In fact, these authors emphasize the element of (unconscious) collusion. This collusion is in contrast to projective identifications in the psychoanalytic and psychotherapeutic situation. Also of interest is that many of the authors' examples are projections of (unwanted) self representations. Since Zinner and colleagues appear to work with a wide variety of patients, this could contradict my earlier generalization that the projection of self representations indicates a primitive process. It is quite possible, however, that the projection of a self representation to a clearly accepting recipient involves a less primitive process than the projection of a self representation to a clearly unwilling recipient.

In the work of Zinner and co-workers, there is no requirement of blurring of self and object representations (step 1-a), although examples are given where the blurring does occur. The reinternalization process (step 3), especially where there is collusion, is not emphasized. However, in the authors' psychotherapeutic work, reinternalization of the projections plays an important role.

PROJECTIVE IDENTIFICATION VERSUS PROJECTION

A few additional words might be useful to clarify further the distinction between projective identification and projection. As already discussed, Kernberg (1987a,b) views projective identification as a more primitive process than projection, one that implies at least some blurring of ego boundaries in the area of the projection. It is this blurring of ego boundaries that causes the projector to hold onto, feel at one with, and continue to identify with the projection. In contrast, projection is seen as occurring when there are clearly differentiated ego boundaries. Here the projector feels little identification with the projection, and may distance himself or herself and stay away from the object of the projection.

Others (Hamilton 1988, Ramchandani 1991) are not in agreement here. They note that in projection proper, there is a clear loss of reality testing, as demonstrated by a conviction that an aspect of the self is in another person. In projective identification, by contrast, the loss of reality testing is not total, as some lack of clarity remains about the location of the self representation. Additionally, projection proper is most characteristic of severely disturbed psychotic patients, whereas projective identification is more characteristic of less disturbed borderline patients. With these differences in mind, projection proper is viewed as a more primitive mechanism than projective identification. The logic behind Hamilton's and Ramchandani's argument is clear. Possibly one might speak of three levels of projection, from most primitive to most advanced: psychotic projection, projective identification, and neurotic projection. Psychotic projection would correspond to the type of projection described by Hamilton and Ramchandani; neurotic projection would correspond to the type of projection described by Kernberg.

With the broadening of the definition of projective identification (with the inclusion of object representations as well as self representations in step 1, and with the elimination of step 1a as a requirement), the distinction between projective identification and projection is less clear. The extreme here is the elimination of the distinction, as in the idea of Malin and Grotstein (1966) that the projector always retains some contact (and identification) with what is projected. In essence, the distinction between projective identification and projection varies in accordance with the definition of projective identification.

POSITIVE PROJECTIVE IDENTIFICATION

All of the examples in this chapter involve projections of negative aspects of the self. Although negative projections predominate in projective identifications, there is also the phenomenon of positive projective identification (Akhtar 1991, Hamilton 1986, 1988). Hamilton provides examples in which psychotic patients project grandiose positive aspects of themselves onto therapists, and then interact with the therapists to induce them to act in accordance with the projections. The therapists who receive such projections might become more optimistic and hopeful about the patients. Likewise there are therapists who project positive attributes of themselves onto psychotic patients who lack these qualities.

Akhtar (1991) speaks of patients who project "undesirable" positive aspects of themselves, that is, positive aspects of themselves that are unwanted. Schizoid and self-loathing individuals, for example, can be uncomfortable with positive traits such as vigor, hope, authenticity, and wit, alleviating themselves of their discomfort by projecting these qualities onto their therapists. Akhtar makes a useful distinction between narcissistic individuals who use negative projective identification, and schizoid and self-loathing individuals who use positive projective identification.

CLINICAL EXAMPLES

Some of the following cases are from psychoanalyses, others from psychotherapy, and still others from interactions outside of psychotherapy. Individuals with neurotic, borderline, and psychotic disorders are all included. The examples show projections of both self representations and object representations. In several cases, there is blurring of ego boundaries. All cases include the interpersonal interaction, where the defenses of identification with the aggressor and the turning of passive into active can be noted. Excerpts from these cases have already been referred to throughout this chapter.

Case 1. Mr. C grew up with a mother who seldom listened to him, who constantly forced her will on him, and who never gave him any choices or alternatives. In regard to all this, Mr. C felt treated unfairly, taken advantage of, and used. As might be expected, he usually viewed his psychoanalyst analogously to his mother. In fact, Mr. C went out of his way to create situations so that he could think of the analyst that way. Additionally, he induced his analyst to act in accordance with his thinking, and then raged at him for his unfair treatment. For example, after clearly agreeing to a policy of paying for missed sessions unless the analyst filled the hour, Mr. C felt that he should not have to pay for an appointment at the time of a rescheduled graduate class. Mr. C assumed that the analyst would charge if he missed and felt taken advantage of and cheated. He repetitively chastised and criticized the analyst about how unfair he was, insisting that the analyst had forced his will on him and would not listen to his point of view. The analyst began to feel both guilty and angry; he felt that maybe he was being unfair to Mr. C and taking advantage of him. He also felt harassed, forced to take the position ascribed to him, and treated poorly by Mr. C. Later it turned out that Mr. C had several other time options regarding the rescheduled class but had neglected to mention them.

In this example, Mr. C projects a maternal object representation onto the analyst, creates situations where he can view the analyst in accordance with this projection, and then tries to force the analyst into accepting the projection.

Case 2. Ms. D, although she functioned in a highly competent fashion and was widely respected in her profession, frequently presented herself in psychoanalysis as inadequate, ineffective, little, and pathetic. She said she was a loser, was inferior to her colleagues, and was looked down upon and scorned by her fellow professionals. Ms. D insisted that her analyst view her in the same way that she saw herself, and repetitively acted to get him to feel and to treat her that way. In a manner particularly annoying to the analyst, Ms. D acted as if it were a fact that the analyst agreed that she was little and inadequate. She elaborated one example after another, based on

> the assumption that the analyst agreed with her. If the analyst made any comment indicating that he felt differently, Ms. D would argue with him and insist that he was being stupid and demeaning. The analyst felt pressured, coerced, overwhelmed, frustrated, and angry.

Here Ms. D retains her self representation as a little, pathetic, devalued professional while projecting onto the analyst an object representation of a demeaning, devaluing, and critical parent. Note that the self representation is retained; it is the object representation (of someone who treats Ms. D in accordance with her self representation) that is projected. Ms. D here interacts very provocatively with the analyst as she tries to get him to accept her projection.

> *Case 3.* As a defense against her own feelings of inadequacy, Dr. E referred to herself in a very exaggerated fashion as an important and knowledgeable member of the senior staff. In charge of making medical rounds, she treated a colleague, Dr. F, as if Dr. F were inadequate. Although Dr. F was almost her equal, Dr. E lectured her and quizzed her as if she were a beginning medical student. When Dr. F did not know something, Dr. E would sigh in disbelief. As this sequence of events continued, Dr. F, also somewhat lacking in self-confidence, began to feel inadequate herself.

This is an example of projective identification outside the psychotherapy setting. Here Dr. E projects a self representation onto Dr. F and then treats Dr. F in accordance with this projection, doing everything possible to make Dr. F accept the unwanted projected feelings.

> *Case 4.* Mr. G, a man with schizophrenia, verbally attacked his therapist. Session after session he yelled and screamed that the therapist was not helping him, that she was worthless and impotent, and that she was incapable of doing anything right. Whatever the therapist did or said, Mr. G immediately jumped

on it as wrong and indicative of her inability to help. As the attacks continued, the therapist began to feel worthless, impotent, and destroyed. Exploration revealed the interaction to be a re-enactment with a role reversal of Mr. G's relationship with his mother, in which he felt worthless and destroyed by her continual verbal attacks on him.

In this case, Mr. G projects a self representation onto his therapist, and then repetitively treats the therapist in accordance with the projection. The therapist begins to view herself in accordance with the projection.

Case 5. Mr. H, a man with a diagnosis of borderline personality disorder, was in a relationship with a highly anxious woman. This man lived from crisis to crisis, yet gave the appearance of utmost calm, that he could deal with anything. He complained bitterly of his girlfriend's high anxiety, yet in telling her about his situations, he would inevitably leave out crucial details, making the situation seem much more dangerous than it actually was. Mr. H would thereby increase his girlfriend's anxiety and then attempt to distance himself from her to get away from the anxiety. Paradoxically, he could not tolerate even a day without contact with her because absence of contact increased his anxiety.

Here is another example of projective identification outside of the psychotherapy session. Here Mr. H rids himself of his anxiety by projecting his self representation onto his girlfriend. In a subtle but clear manner, he relates to his girlfriend in a way that induces her to feel and act in accordance with the projection. In this case, the blurring of self and object representations is noted by Mr. H's unclarity about who is anxious, himself or his girlfriend. There is a blurring of an anxious self representation with an anxious object representation. This blurring is also evident in Mr. H's inability to make this projection totally, as shown by his need for daily contact with his girlfriend.

Case 6. Mr. I, a man with a diagnosis of paranoid schizophrenia, had difficulty writing his check at the end of one session. He could not spell words; he could not remember the date or to whom to write the check. Obviously in a disorganized state, he said to the therapist that he was dangerous and bad, and that she had better watch out or he would mess up her thought processes. He then started acting in a very disorganized and disruptive manner. He told the therapist that she was rigid and inflexible as he was going over his hour; then he reversed himself and said no, it was he who was rigid and inflexible. He called the therapist bad names; then he said maybe it was he rather than she who was bad. He said he did not ever want to see the therapist again, yet had a hard time leaving. When he left, the therapist felt very unsettled and disorganized herself.

This is a case where a disorganized self representation is projected onto the therapist. By being exposed to the ramifications of Mr. I's disorganization, the therapist is left feeling that same way herself. In this case, the blurring of self and object representations is most clear: Mr. I has difficulty distinguishing himself from the therapist.

6

THE DEPRESSIVE IMPULSE-RIDDEN CHARACTER AND THE CORE BORDERLINE PERSONALITY

This chapter describes a type of borderline patient, termed the *depressive impulse-ridden character,* and differentiates this patient from a more disturbed borderline individual, termed the *core borderline personality.* There is a group of patients, appearing somewhat frequently in psychotherapy practices today, who meet the *DSM-IV* diagnostic criteria for the borderline personality disorder, yet might not be considered borderline individuals by other, more psychodynamic diagnostic approaches. Unlike the borderline patients described by Kernberg (1967, 1975, 1976, 1980, 1984) or by the ego-psychological diagnostic approach, these individuals always maintain reality testing and do not display identity diffusion. Although primitive defenses are used, these defenses are utilized in a different and less prominent pattern than by other borderline individuals. Like most borderline patients, these individuals display marked problems in impulse control and frustration tolerance, plus affective instability. Beneath a superficial appearance of decent interpersonal relations and adaptation, there are obvious and characteristic problems.

Because this group of individuals organizes its identity in accordance with a "bad self," and because its impulsivity is marked and characteristic, this group will here be called *depressive impulse-ridden characters.*

THE CORE BORDERLINE PERSONALITY

Before elaborating about the depressive impulse-ridden character, the core borderline personality, somewhat modeled after the work of Kernberg, will be discussed. In making the borderline diagnosis, Kernberg has placed most emphasis on three ego functions: the proclivity to use primitive defenses, the syndrome of identity diffusion, and the relative ability to maintain reality testing. Regarding reality testing, my emphasis is slightly different from that of Kernberg, in that my focus is on the vulnerability for regression rather than the relative intactness.

Individuals diagnosed borderline by a selective focus on reality testing, defenses, and identity will invariably show the overall borderline ego profile as outlined by the ego-psychological diagnostic approach. If one insists on the demonstration of these three ego weaknesses to make the diagnosis, individuals diagnosed this way would have rather marked psychopathology. I use the term *core borderline personality* to refer to these individuals.

THE DEPRESSIVE IMPULSE-RIDDEN CHARACTER

In contrast to the core borderline personality, the depressive impulse-ridden character is not characterized by any of the three core ego weaknesses just discussed. Yet, these individuals certainly would be diagnosed borderline by *DSM-IV*. The depressive impulse-ridden character organizes his identity in accordance with a "bad self." This individual views himself as inadequate, inept, of little worth and value, sometimes even as harmful. To feel decent about himself, he usually has to live up to certain difficult internalized aspirations, ideals, and achievements, and in addition, receive repetitive external positive feedback from others. In accordance with this he often seeks out and forms relationships where he can obtain this needed positive feedback. At times, these need-fulfilling relationships can become clinging, demanding, and controlling. Even when feeling adequate about himself on the surface, the identity of the "bad self" is operational at a preconscious or unconscious level, motivating behavior. Various activities and acting-out behaviors are used to ward off painful affects associated with this identity. These include the use of alcohol and drugs, sexual and antisocial behavior, and many kinds of compulsive behaviors, not all of which are necessarily destructive.

In relation to the activation of the "bad self," impulsive behavior can be self-directed and self-destructive. Sometimes an unconscious desire for punishment can result in a variety of masochistic, dangerous, and self-defeating behaviors. Related to a vulnerability associated with the identity of the "bad self," there is almost always a sensitivity to negative feedback, slights, and rejections, with a particular difficulty in frustration tolerance and impulse control in this area.

The identity based on the "bad self," although very pathological, is certainly cohesive and stable, clearly in contrast to identity diffusion, where there is a series of multiple contradictory identities. The identity based on the "bad self" also appears less pathological than that of the narcissistic personality. This "bad self" identity is usually established early in life, certainly beginning in the preoedipal years. Often it is related to environments where the individual was consistently treated as if he were not worth much, certainly not unless he lived up to certain difficult standards or expectations. This could be overtly or covertly conveyed by the parents, or related to early environments where the child was neglected.

Regarding defenses, although the depressive impulse-ridden character has the proclivity to use some of the more primitive defenses, especially under stress, the use of these defenses has a different and lesser pattern than that of the core borderline personality. Regarding Kernberg's borderline defenses of splitting, primitive idealization, devaluation, primitive denial, projection, and projective identification, the depressive impulse-ridden character has much less tendency than the core borderline personality to use these in day-to-day functioning. Here the depressive impulse-ridden character more commonly uses a combination of neurotic and immature defenses, with a propensity to utilize acting out and externalization. However, under stress, the borderline defenses are more frequently employed. Even here, however, the depressive impulse-ridden character, in comparison to the core borderline personality, has the capacity more easily to reverse these defenses spontaneously.

Regarding reality testing, the depressive impulse-ridden character differs from the core borderline personality in that this ego function is basically always intact. Although there can be subtle distortions in reality testing in relation to the activation of primitive defenses or to the tendency to see the present day in relation to infantile fantasies and infantile self images, there are no actual psychotic episodes.

Diagnosing by the ego-psychological diagnostic approach, as elaborated in Chapter 1, one could say that, despite the absence of the three core weaknesses, the depressive impulse-ridden character fits best in the borderline group. Summarizing the ego strengths and weaknesses, the depressive impulse-ridden character is characterized by good reality testing and secondary-process thinking, without much propensity to regress in those areas under stress. Interpersonal relations are maintained on a superficial level, yet are basically need-fulfilling, and often can become clinging, demanding, and controlling. Adaptation to reality is maintained on the surface, but under the influence of other ego problems, is usually far from optimal. Regarding defenses, in day-to-day functioning the depressive impulse-ridden character basically uses a combination of neurotic and immature defenses. The defenses of acting out and externalization deserve special mention here. Under stress, there is a marked tendency additionally to use borderline defenses. The depressive impulse-ridden character is organized around an identity in accordance with a "bad self." Although highly pathological, this identity is cohesive and stable, in marked contrast to that of identity diffusion. Partially under the influence of this identity and the feeling states that accompany it, there are marked problems in impulse control and frustration tolerance, together with affective instability.

At this point, I might stress what is obvious, that the depressive impulse-ridden character can be thought of as consisting of two essential elements: the depressive element and the impulse-ridden element. The depressive element makes depressive impulse-ridden characters similar to individuals described in the literature as having "depressive" personalities, or to individuals described as very susceptible to depression. The description of the manic-depressive personality (Cohen et al. 1954) from the workers at Chestnut Lodge is quite relevant here. Additionally, the personality core of depressed individuals, elaborated by Leo Stone (1986) might be mentioned, in addition to Kernberg's (1971) discussion of various types of depressive personalities. It is the impulse-ridden element that differentiates the depressive impulse-ridden character from these other "depressive" characters and brings the borderline diagnosis into question.

NARROW VERSUS BROAD CLASSIFICATIONS

The differentiation of the depressive impulse-ridden character from the core borderline personality leads to a discussion of narrow versus broad diagnostic classifications (Goldstein

1989b). I am currently in disagreement with some of the experts about this area. Although there might be some support for my perspective (Waldinger 1993), there is general agreement among a number of experts (Gunderson 1984, Meissner 1984, Stone 1987) that Kernberg's concept of the borderline personality organization (requiring identity diffusion plus the use of borderline defenses) provides a broad classification, whereas *DSM-IV* and Gunderson (1984) offer a narrower classification. I think this is incorrect. In essence, I think that these experts view Kernberg's concept of the borderline personality as broader than it actually is, while they correspondingly view Gunderson's and the *DSM-IV* criteria as narrower than they in fact are.

Viewing Kernberg's classification as a broad one is possibly based on the premise that patients who show even mild problems in identity suffer from identity diffusion, plus the associated premise that the miscellaneous use of borderline defenses is sufficient to qualify for a weakness in the area of defense. In contrast to this, in accordance with Kernberg, I consider identity diffusion to be present only when there is a clear lack of an integrated and stable self-concept, and a corresponding lack of an integrated and stable concept of objects. The problem of identity diffusion is severe and not necessarily characteristic of the vast majority of patients diagnosed as borderline.

Likewise, regarding defenses, I do not consider the occasional use of a borderline defense as indicating weakness in this area. Everyone uses a little denial and splitting. In contrast, a patient with an ego weakness in defenses should display either a clearly increased use of primitive defenses in day-to-day functioning or a marked tendency to rely on these defenses under stress. Again, this indicates significant psychopathology and is not necessarily characteristic of the vast majority of patients diagnosed as borderline.

We now turn to Gunderson's concept of borderline personality disorder and to the *DSM-IV* borderline diagnostic criteria. Both Gunderson and *DSM-IV* view the borderline personality disorder as one of many personality disorders, all distinguishable from each other. Theoretically, this goes along with a narrow classification. The problem is that the diagnostic criteria of both Gunderson and *DSM-IV* do not seem to be in accordance with this. For example, there appears to be considerable overlap between the *DSM-IV* borderline personality disorder and many of the other *DSM-IV* personality disorders. This especially applies to many *DSM-IV* histrionic, antisocial, narcissistic, schizotypal, paranoid, and schizoid personality disorders, but sometimes to others as well. Although the intent is to provide a narrow classification, neither *DSM-IV* nor Gunderson's criteria appear to accomplish that.

The ego-psychological diagnostic approach can provide either a broad or a narrow classification of the borderline patient. This will depend on how many and which of the ego weaknesses are required to make the diagnosis. For example, if identity diffusion, the proclivity to use primitive ego defenses, and the propensity to regress in reality testing are all required to establish the borderline diagnosis, this then would provide a narrow classification. If, however, as suggested in Chapter 1, one looks at the overall pattern of ego strengths and weaknesses and establishes into which large grouping (the normal-neurotic, the narcissistic, the borderline, or the psychotic) a patient best fits, then this would provide a broad classification.

CLINICAL EXAMPLES

To help bring the depressive impulse-ridden character to life, this chapter will conclude with two clinical examples.

> Ms. B, a 27-year-old woman, was hospitalized briefly after superficially cutting her wrist. In response to a fight with her boyfriend, who told her that he no longer wanted to see her, Ms. B had initially become enraged. However, after she had

thrown a few ashtrays, her intense anger subsided. She remained in her apartment, watching television, but could not concentrate on the show. Instead, she began to brood about her boyfriend's rejection. She began to think that if he did not like her, she must not be worth much. She increasingly thought of herself as unlovable and ugly, with little potential to live up to her goal of getting married. She began to feel worthless, as if she were a very bad person.

Ms. B had very frequently experienced similar painful feelings, and had often used marijuana or excessive alcohol to help diminish the discomfort. On this occasion, however, she responded by impulsively cutting her wrist. Subsequently, she wound up on the psychiatry service at a local hospital, marking her third hospital admission of this nature.

Ms. B was particularly sensitive to slights and rebuffs. It was almost always this type of insult that precipitated the activation of her self-image of inadequacy, ugliness, worthlessness, and sometimes even evilness. Concomitantly there was often the image of the one who "hurt" her as an all-bad enemy. With the help of regular positive feedback from co-workers and customers who admired her talents as a hairstylist, Ms. B was usually able to feel fairly good about herself. In addition, the praise of current boyfriends, often chosen unconsciously for their tendencies to admire her and dote over her, shored up Ms. B's self-image. However, the image of herself as a bad person was always beneath the surface and ready for easy activation.

This image (of a bad self) was based on Ms. B's early upbringing. Ms. B was the fourth daughter and clearly unwanted. She was physically abused by her mother, and received positive feedback from her parents only when she performed exceptionally. Her self-concept was obviously pathological, yet integrated, consistent, and stable. It was often suppressed or repressed, but easily evoked. When present, it stimulated the pattern of impulsive acting out and affective instability, in addition to the use of primitive defense. Even when beneath the surface, this "bad self" image influenced Ms. B in her choice of troubled and needy male friends.

Ms. D, a 33-year-old lawyer, sought treatment because she felt very much at the mercy of her changing affect states. She performed well in the structured setting of her law office, yet often felt "out of control" when outside this location. She was frequently subject to promiscuity and drinking spells, and was drawn to somewhat dangerous sports, like sky diving and mountain climbing. Her pattern with men involved an attraction to rather sensual but troubled individuals, often heavy drinkers, almost always beneath her intellectually. A typical relationship involved much drinking, mutually exciting sex, and a rapid end of the relationship. When Ms. D was working diligently at the office or involved in "stimulating" activities, she felt good about herself and her life, displaying a pleasant appearance and affect. She was a very talented lawyer, and because of this, obtained a fair amount of praise and admiration at the office. Additionally, her numerous social contacts, although usually superficial and short-lived, provided positive feedback.

It was when Ms. D had "free" time or was alone that she got into trouble. When this occurred, she had a tendency to focus her attention on herself, to dwell on something that had recently happened at the office, and to question her performance. An unpleasant image of herself as flawed and deficient, especially compared to others, gradually would emerge. She would begin to view herself as unattractive, unlovable, and somewhat worthless. This would precipitate a very painful feeling, one which Ms. D typically tried to counteract by drinking, by physical activity, sexual escapades, or "exciting" sports. This "bad self" image, although clearly pathological, was consistent, consolidated, and cohesive.

This image was related to an early history of being the scapegoat of the family. Ms. D had been constantly devalued compared to her more attractive older sister, and then almost dropped entirely by her parents as an object of affection when her younger brother was born. Praise, admiration, and even acknowledgment were very lacking in Ms. D's early life. In order to gain some positive feedback, Ms. D, at a very early age, began competing actively in sports, mostly with boys in the neighborhood. Although this did not particularly please her parents, it helped Ms. D receive "attention" from her peers. She also became an involved and very successful student, attaining more substantial acknowledgment from this endeavor. Her pattern of multiple activities and a busy schedule was thus established very early in life.

Negative feedback was not necessary for Ms. D to evoke the image of herself as a bad person. Merely being alone was usually all that was needed. Under the influence of this "bad self" image, frustration tolerance was minimal, and affective lability and instability were prominent. Ms. D was prone to impulse-ridden and dangerous activities at these times. Although she utilized acting out, Ms. D did not use more typical borderline defenses, even under stress. Her typical day-to-day defenses included reaction formation, isolation, rationalization, and externalization. Reality testing and thought processes were always maintained.

7

DIFFERENT CONCEPTS OF THE BORDERLINE PATIENT

This chapter succinctly reviews some of the historical and current concepts of the borderline patient. It should demonstrate the usefulness of the ego-psychological diagnostic approach in understanding these different concepts and also provide brief summaries of different experts' ideas about the borderline patient.

ZILBOORG

Zilboorg (1941) described a group of patients called *ambulatory schizophrenics* who, although they were able to participate in life in a way that seemed somewhat normal, under scrutiny showed subtle defects that indicated a schizophrenic process. Zilboorg described these patients as taciturn and somewhat autistic, with tendencies to establish shallow interpersonal relations, with difficulty establishing long-term goal-directed pursuits, with overwhelming amounts of anger (although often not directly expressed), with chronic tenseness and anxiety, with tendencies to intellectualize, with tendencies to overindulge in alcohol, and with simple and inhibited sexual lives. Although Zilboorg considered these patients to be schizophrenic, some of them would probably be called borderline by the ego-psychological diagnostic approach. Those not actually schizophrenic would fall into the more pathological end of the borderline spectrum.

HOCH AND POLATIN

Hoch and Polatin (1949) described a group of patients called *pseudoneurotic schizophrenics* who showed a clinical pattern of pananxiety, panneurosis, and pansexuality. Although these individuals appeared highly neurotic, the authors felt that close scrutiny revealed schizophrenia. Besides the core symptoms, these patients were described as displaying a lack of modulation and flexibility in emotions, emotional coldness, hypersensitivity to emotional situations, plus open hatred. Hoch and Polatin deemed these patients to be schizophrenic because of basically autistic lifestyles, greater than neurotic amounts of ambivalence, affects subtly lacking in modulation and flexibility, and subtle signs of thinking disturbances. Today, some of these patients might fit into the borderline group by the ego-psychological diagnostic approach. Like the ambulatory schizophrenics of Zilboorg, these patients would fall into the more pathological end of the borderline spectrum.

BYCHOWSKY

Bychowsky (1953) described a group of patients called *latent psychotics* who did not appear psychotic on the surface, yet had the potential to regress and become psychotic under stress. These patients were described as having too much primary process in their productions, the vulnerability to regression and overreaction to frustration, primitive megalomania, the use of primitive defenses, magical thinking, ideas of reference, evidence of poor development of ego boundaries, and primitive, unsublimated, nonneutralized aggression. On the surface these individuals often looked neurotic, socially deviant, or characterological. Although many of these patients were probably basically psychotic as Bychowsky contended, some might fit into the borderline group by the ego-psychological diagnostic approach, again at the more pathological end of the spectrum.

STERN

Stern (1938) was the first to use the term *borderline.* He differed from Zilboorg, Hoch and Polatin, and Bychowsky in that he did not view his patient as basically psychotic, but rather, as having a kind of stable psychopathology, somewhere between the neuroses and the psychoses. In this conceptualization, he predated Kernberg by a number of years. Stern characterized his patients by ten features: narcissism, psychic bleeding, inordinate hypersensitivity, psychic rigidity, negative therapeutic reactions, feelings of inferiority, masochism, somatic insecurity or anxiety, the use of projective mechanisms, and subtle difficulties in reality testing. Differential diagnosis in Stern's patients appear to be more between borderline and neurotic than between borderline and psychotic. In some ways, these patients resemble Kohut's narcissistic personalities. Nevertheless, Stern's group would basically meet the ego-psychological diagnostic criteria for the borderline diagnosis.

DEUTSCH

Deutsch (1942) described a group of patients called *as-if personalities* who on the surface appeared normal, but who nevertheless suffered from marked emotional impoverishment and pathology of their internalized object relations. These patients had lives that seemed lacking in genuineness, with interpersonal relationships that were devoid of warmth, concern, and empathy. These people acted *as-if* they were normal, yet beneath this facade they were clearly troubled. They also tended to adopt the qualities of whomever they had contact with, acting *as-if* they were the other person. These people were further characterized by their suggestibility, their marked passivity, and their feelings of depersonalization and derealization. Like Stern, Deutsch viewed these individuals as having a kind of stable psychopathology, somewhere between the neuroses and psychoses in severity. These patients would clearly fit into the borderline group when applying the ego-psychological diagnostic approach. With their marked problems in identity, these patients probably would meet the criteria for core borderline personalities.

KNIGHT

Knight (1953) followed Stern in actually using the term *borderline.* He focused on patients who used both neurotic and psychotic mechanisms, had not yet "broken with reality," but who demonstrated sufficient maladjustment and ominous clinical signs to preclude the diagnosis of psychoneurosis. Knight strongly emphasized an evaluation of ego functions in making the borderline diagnosis. His patients demonstrated superficial adaptation to the environment, superficial maintenance of interpersonal relationships, and intact reality testing on the surface. Knight compiled lists of what he called macroscopic and microscopic evidence of ego weakness. Macroscopic weaknesses included the lack of concern over the predicament, an absence of observable precipitating stresses, a viewing of the symptoms as ego syntonic or externally precipitated, the lack of achievement over time, unrealistic planning, the relating of bizarre dreams, and insufficient contrast between dreams and waking life. Microscopic evidence included impaired integration of ideas, impaired concept formation, impaired judgment, occasional blocking, peculiarities of word usage, obliviousness to obvious implications, contamination of idioms, occasional inappropriate affect, suspicion-laden questions and behavior, and lack of recognition of and embarrassment over peculiarities of speech. The emphasis on such a variety of ego impairments makes one suspect that a number of Knight's patients were basically psychotic. Others, however, might fit into the borderline category via the ego-psychological diagnostic approach, at the psychotic end of the spectrum.

FROSCH

Frosch (1964, 1970) described a specific group of patients called *psychotic characters.* Again, these individuals demonstrated a level of stable psychopathology between the neuroses and the psychoses. Barring certain features, these people would be psychotic, and in fact, they could regress to psychoses at times of stress. What distinguished these patients from the psychotics was their relative ability to preserve reality testing, their superior object relations, their capacity for rapid reversibility when regressions did occur, and the presence of reality-syntonic adaptations. Frosch's emphasis on a specific and stable intermediate level of psychopathology was like that of his predecessors—Stern, Deutsch, and Knight—and clearly previewed Kernberg's concept. His patients would clearly fall into the borderline group via the ego-psychological diagnostic approach, meeting the criteria for core borderline personalities.

KERNBERG

Kernberg (1967, 1975, 1976, 1980, 1984) uses the term *borderline personality organization* to refer to a group of patients with a specific, stable pathological personality organization, distinct from both the more pathological psychotic organization and the less pathological neurotic organization. It was Kernberg's work that was most influential in the elaboration of the borderline concept of the ego-psychological diagnostic approach. As noted, I use the term *core borderline personality* to refer to the borderline group specifically detailed by Kernberg. Regarding Kernberg's work, it continues to offer an integration and synthesis of earlier writings, plus a unified and comprehensive framework for description, definition, and understanding. It was Kernberg's work that provided the impetus for the acceptance and popularization of the term *borderline.*

MASTERSON AND RINSLEY

Masterson (1976, 1978, 1981) and Rinsley (1977, 1978, 1989) described a specific group of borderline patients, very similar to those of Kernberg. In multiple articles and books, these authors elaborated in detail on basically all aspects of the borderline patient. They complemented Kernberg's work by focusing on what actually transpired in early life between the potential borderline child and his parents. They emphasized a process whereby the mother, deriving much gratification from the symbiotic involvement with the child, withdrew her emotional availability when the child began to separate and individuate. This process peaked at the rapprochement subphase (16 to 25 months) of separation-individuation, presenting the child with the dilemma of being faced with a rejecting, disapproving, and withdrawing (bad) mother when he strove for age-appropriate growth, and a comforting (good) mother when he remained dependent, passive, and compliant. This led to the internalization of the "split object relations unit," the hallmark of the borderline patient. Masterson and Rinsley later broadened their etiological concept to include constitutional defects, maternal unavailability for separation-individuation regardless of the cause, and other stresses related to the separation-individuation process. Their patients would clearly fall into the borderline category of the ego-psychological diagnostic approach, also meeting the criteria for core borderline patients.

MEISSNER

Meissner's (1984, 1988, 1993) concept of the borderline spectrum has already been discussed and incorporated into the ego-psychological diagnostic approach. Meissner divides his borderline spectrum into two continua, the hysterical and the schizoid. The hysterical continuum listed in decreasing order of psychopathology, includes the pseudoschizophrenic group, the psychotic character, the dysphoric personality, and the primitive hysteric. The schizoid continuum includes the schizoid personality, the as-if personality, the false-self organization, and the condition of identity diffusion. Although the subgroups of the hysterical continuum are well differentiated from one another, there is some unclarity about one of these subgroups, the primitive hysteric. The subgroups of the schizoid continuum do not seem well differentiated from each other and possibly represent different ways of viewing the same entity. Meissner's view of the borderline conditions as a heterogeneous spectrum of levels and degrees of pathological personality functioning is an excellent and very useful conceptualization. The grouping of this spectrum into two continua and the specifics of these continua, however, is more questionable.

ABEND, PORDER, AND WILLICK

Abend, Porder, and Willick (1983) wrote a book describing in detail the classical psychoanalyses of four borderline patients. Based on a discussion with twenty-five of their colleagues over a 4-year period, they detailed descriptive features of borderline patients. With regard to the ego-psychological diagnostic approach, there was no mention of problems in frustration tolerance and impulse control, and no mention of severe problems in identity. In addition, these authors generally described their patients as functioning at a higher defensive level than often attributed to borderline patients. Regarding interpersonal relations, Abend and co-workers focused on disturbances often associated with more neurotic individuals, including oedipal problems, sadomasochistic relationships, superego conflicts, and narcissistic problems. Although defects in reality testing were noted, these defects did not include actual regressions to self and object dedifferentiation. Problems in adaptation to reality and in affective instability were noted, as were polysymptomatic clinical representations and the prominence of aggressive conflicts. Although these patients evidenced clear psychopathology, they seem healthier than most borderline patients described. Regarding the ego-psychological diagnostic approach, these patients appear to be on the healthiest end of the spectrum.

KOHUT

Kohut (1971, 1977, 1984) described a group of patients, the narcissistic personalities, whom he saw as distinctly healthier than borderline individuals. He characterized these patients as having structural configurations that were stable and cohesive, although primitive and archaic. According to Kohut, the stability and cohesiveness of these narcissistic configurations allowed these patients to resist disruptive fragmentation and to undergo successful psychoanalyses.

These patients often present with symptoms or complaints that tend to be vague and ill defined. With exploration, it is noted that these individuals have highly labile self-esteem, being exceedingly sensitive to perceived slights, rejections, rebuffs, disappointments, and failures. These "insults" often produce uncomfortable feeling states such as rage, humiliation, embarrassment, and shame, with compensatory defensive behavior, sometimes quite destructive. Additionally, there are often problems in sexuality (perverse fantasies and/or lack of sexual interest), in social relations (work inhibitions, lacks in interpersonal relations, delinquency), in the manifest personality (lack of humor, lack of empathy, lack of sense of proportion), and in the psychosomatic sphere (hypochondriasis).

These patients are clearly healthier than the core borderline personalities. When viewed in accordance with the ego-psychological diagnostic approach in the broad sense, some of these patients might fit into the borderline spectrum, clearly at the healthiest end of the continuum. I view many of these narcissistic patients as distinctly different from borderline patients, warranting a separate structural configuration.

STONE

Stone (1988) describes a group of patients characterized by a heightened central-nervous-system irritability. These patients present childhoods characterized by restlessness, tantrums, irascibility, impatience, and demandingness. In adolescence, these qualities might persist, or give way to moodiness, poor self-discipline, and marked impulsivity. In adulthood, mood fluctuations become more apparent. Problems in frustration tolerance and impulse control are evidenced, as these patients frequently overreact to mild stimuli and then have difficulty stopping their reactions. Additionally, these individuals are often "sensation seeking," looking for stimulation to ward off dysphoric feelings such as apathy and boredom. Identity problems also present themselves, along with tendencies to use primitive defenses, plus certain dissociative phenomena.

Although identity problems and primitive defenses are noted by Stone, these are seen as secondary to the hyperirritability. When the former are marked, these patients present as core borderline personalities. However, many of these individuals are better classified as depressive impulse-ridden characters.

ADLER AND BUIE

Adler and Buie (Adler 1985, 1993, Adler and Buie 1979, Buie and Adler 1982–1983) describe a group of borderline patients whose core problem is hypothesized to be a defect in a specific kind of introject, the holding introject. According to Adler and Buie, in normal development, the mother, in the capacity of a selfobject, supplies holding and soothing. By 8 months, when the child attains recognition memory, if there has been good-enough mothering, he can begin to use transitional objects to provide holding and soothing in the mother's absence. At around 18 months, with the attainment of evocative memory, the holding and soothing previously provided only by selfobjects and transitional objects can be internalized as holding introjects. In borderline patients, the mother does not provide adequate holding and soothing. Because of this lack, the child cannot use transitional objects for this function, nor is he ever able to internalize holding introjects. He thus remains dependent throughout life on external objects (i.e., other people) to provide the needed holding and soothing. The borderline patients described by Adler and Buie can be classified as core borderline personalities.

GUNDERSON AND WALDINGER

Based on the results of a series of empirical investigations, Gunderson (1984) modified his original lists of characteristic features of borderline patients (Gunderson and Kolb 1978, Gunderson and Singer 1975). In rank order of importance, Gunderson cites seven characteristics: intense unstable interpersonal relationships, manipulative suicide attempts, unstable sense of self, negative affects, ego-dystonic psychotic experiences, impulsivity, and low achievement. Gunderson notes that devaluation, manipulation, dependency, and masochism characterize and cause the intensity and instability of the interpersonal relationships. Additionally, he cites intolerance of aloneness and abandonment anxiety as phenomena closely related to the unstable sense of self.

Gunderson classifies his group of patients as suffering from the borderline personality disorder as opposed to Kernberg's borderline personality organization. Despite the fact that both groups seem somewhat similar, Gunderson believes that the borderline personality disorder represents only a fraction of those patients considered to have the borderline personality organization, as defined by Kernberg. Gunderson believes that the borderline personality disorder is one of many types of severe personality disorders. This is in contrast to Kernberg's borderline personality organization, which Gunderson feels is a broader classification, basically including all severe personality disorders.

Waldinger and Gunderson (1987) described in detail the

treatment of five borderline patients. All appeared to be very difficult patients, with at least three fitting into the category of the core borderline personality.

LIEBOWITZ AND KLEIN

Liebowitz and Klein (1981) describe a group of patients called *hysteroid dysphorics.* These patients are characterized by intolerance of personal rejections (with particularly severe vulnerability to losses of romantic attachment); brief, painful, depressive, crash-like reactions to personal rejections; dysphoric responses to rejections characterized by overeating, oversleeping, or fatigue; self-esteem that is dependent on constant external approval; and the ability to be brought out of the depressive reactions by attention and approval. These patients are often histrionic, flamboyant, intrusive, seductive, self-centered, demanding, and overconcerned with appearance. They can abuse substances, show poor judgment, and act out easily.

These hysteroid dysphorics seem to have a combination of depressive, histrionic, and narcissistic features. Some appear to fit into the borderline group, when viewed in accordance with the ego-psychological diagnostic approach in the broad sense. Most of these patients are not core borderline personalities.

VOLKAN

Volkan (1987) describes six steps in the treatment of "psychoses-prone" borderline patients, based on his experiences of long-term psychoanalytic treatment with nine of these patients. He describes these patients as suffering from identity diffusion, using primitive defenses, and displaying regressions in reality testing. Additionally, these patients are characterized by problems in frustration tolerance and impulse control, affective instability, and by troubled and chaotic relationships. Certainly these patients warrant the borderline diagnosis by the ego-psychological diagnostic approach, basically falling into the category of core borderline personalities.

GIOVACCHINI

Giovacchini (1984, 1993a,b, Goldstein 1994) prefers the term *character disorder* to that of *borderline.* He uses this term to describe any patient whose main psychopathology is expressed in terms of defects in psychic structure. Based on developmental level, he divides character disorders into several groups. The most primitive of these are the schizoid states. These patients have their difficulties originating in the earliest months of life, at a time Giovacchini calls the prementational phase. Giovacchini conceptualizes these patients as having a psyche without intermediary links, without bridges or connections between lower and upper levels of the psychic apparatus. Empty spaces in the psyche are somatically organized and devoid of psychological content. Borderline states are a little less primitive than the schizoid personalities. These patients move toward the world rather than away, but they do it in an awkward and inept way. They are deficient in technique and knowledge, and are lacking in basic structure and self-esteem. A little less primitive are the character neuroses. These patients have a repertoire of adaptive defensive techniques and often adjust adequately on a superficial level. However, they respond to stress by either anxiety and feelings of inadequacy or by narcissistic defenses.

All of these patients present with fragmented personalities and defective self representations; they have problems adapting to the external world and establishing interpersonal relationships. They are basically concrete and mechanistic in their thinking and display structural defects and discontinuities. These patients fit into the borderline group by the ego psychological diagnostic approach, at the lower end of the borderline spectrum.

DSM-IV

To make the *DSM-IV* (1994) diagnosis of borderline personality disorder, there needs to be a "pervasive pattern of instability of interpersonal relationships, self-image and affects, and marked impulsivity beginning in early adulthood and present in a variety of contexts." One must demonstrate at least five of nine items on a checklist to establish the diagnosis. These items are (1) frantic efforts to avoid real or imagined abandonment, (2) a pattern of unstable and intense interpersonal relationships characterized or alternating between extremes of idealization and devaluation, (3) identity disturbance, (4) impulsivity in at least two areas that are potentially self-disparaging, (5) recurrent suicidal behavior, gestures, or self-mutilating behavior, (6) affective instability due to marked reactivity of mood, (7) chronic feelings of emptiness, (8) inappropriate, intense anger or difficulty controlling anger, and (9) transient, stress-related paranoid ideation or severe dissociative symptoms.

Like Gunderson, *DSM-IV* views the borderline personality as one of many different personality disorders. This is in contrast to the ego-psychological diagnostic approach, which views the borderline individual as one of four supraordinate diagnoses, differentiated by structural configurations. Although theoretically different, the ego-psychological diagnostic approach is totally compatible with *DSM-IV*.

Part II

PSYCHOTHERAPY

8

OVERVIEW OF PSYCHOTHERAPY

The different types of psychotherapy can be conceptualized on a continuum, with the most insight-oriented and exploratory types at one end and the most supportive types at the other (Goldstein 1985, 1988a). Five types of psychotherapy along this continuum will be examined: psychoanalysis, analytically oriented psychotherapy, modified analytically oriented psychotherapy, dynamically oriented psychotherapy, and supportive psychotherapy. There is a rich and vast literature (Bibring 1954, Dewald 1971, Gill 1954, Kernberg 1980, Stone 1951, 1954, Tarachow 1963, Ticho 1970, Wallerstein 1965) differentiating some of these different types of psychotherapies, particular psychoanalysis and the analytically oriented psychotherapies. This chapter does not attempt to explore this literature in any detail, but rather, describes and differentiates the various kinds of psychotherapy in an abbreviated way.

PSYCHOANALYSIS

The trappings of psychoanalysis involve the patient's coming for regularly scheduled sessions, four or five times a week, for a number of years. There is no contact between patient and psychoanalyst outside of the appointments. Sessions are conducted with the patient lying on the psychoanalytic couch and the analyst sitting comfortably behind the patient. The patient is instructed simply to free associate; that is, he is to do his best to say whatever comes to his mind and not eliminate any thoughts for any reason. He is particularly cautioned to try not to eliminate thoughts because he thinks they are silly or irrelevant, because he is fearful that the analyst will disapprove, because he wants to avoid uncomfortable feelings associated with them, or because the thoughts relate to the analyst. Often this is all the instruction the patient is given.

As the patient tries to free associate, various resistances within him make the process difficult. As these resistances are noticed by the analyst, he will comment on them in an effort to help the patient overcome them and continue to free associate. The analyst initially confines his comments to these resistances and to helping the patient to elaborate and expand on what he is saying. Throughout the psychoanalysis the analyst's comments remain of a very specific nature. They are directed specifically to the analytic process and are almost always in the nature of clarifications and interpretations. Almost all comments serve the singular purpose of enhancing the psychoanalytic process. Psychoanalysis works as a very gradual process during which aspects of oneself that were previously unconscious become conscious. The transference is used as the primary and most effective forum for this process. In order to provide a setting in which the patient can most easily transfer his feelings onto the analyst, the analyst has to be seen in a neutral way. It is for this reason that the analyst confines his remarks to clarifications and interpretations regarding the psychoanalytic process as exclusively as possible. The analyst is thus able to maintain his "neutral" position while still being warm, empathic, and concerned about the patient.

Aided by the frequency and the intensity of the sessions, by the use of the couch and the basic process of free association, and by the maintenance of a neutral position by the analyst, a progressively intense transference becomes established. This intense transference involves the patient, in a regressed state, displacing or "transferring" onto the analyst feelings and thoughts that were originally directed toward the important people of his early childhood. The transference includes not only these feelings and thoughts, but also defenses against them. It is based on both the actual and fantasized past, as experienced by the patient. The patient's pathological and nonpathological personality traits, as well as his symptoms, all based on intrapsychic conflict, are activated in the psychoanalytic process and become an integral part of the transference. It is the establishment and working through of the transference that is crucial to the attainment of insight, and that most clearly differentiates psychoanalysis from other forms of psychotherapy.

Continuing to confine himself basically to clarifications and interpretations, the analyst begins to comment on aspects of the transference about which the patient is unaware, especially when these appear as resistances to the analytic process. He correlates what is happening in the transference with the patient's current interactions and relationships with significant others, and especially with the patient's significant interactions and relationships in childhood. In this way the analyst helps the patient to begin to learn about previously unconscious aspects of himself, including those aspects that have afforded him the most difficulty. As the patient expands his awareness in this way and gains insight, he is gradually able to make adaptive adjustments and changes in his psychopathology, in his personality, and in his life. The permanency of these changes can be attributed to underlying "structural change," that is, changes in the alignment and relationship of the id, ego, and superego. The analytic process is not smooth; rather, it is characterized by continual resistances and continual progressions and regressions, but with a gradual overall advancement.

Gill (1954), in his classic paper, defined psychoanalysis as a therapeutic technique employed by a neutral analyst that permits and results in the development of an intense regressive transference, with the ultimate resolution of this transference by the technique of interpretation alone. There are basically three aspects of this definition that distinguish analysis from other forms of psychotherapy: the analyst's neutrality, the development and resolution of the transference, and the emphasis on interpretation as the primary therapeutic intervention. It is these three aspects that many (Kernberg 1980, Ticho 1970) focus on when differentiating psychoanalysis from other forms of psychotherapy. Given this definition, for analysis to be successful, the patient's personality traits, symptoms, and psychopathology must become activated in the treatment situation, enter into a specific transference with the analyst, and be worked through and resolved in the analytic process by interpretation alone. Thus, a critical criterion for analyzability is that such a transference can be formed and resolved without disruptive fragmentation or regression. The basically neurotic individual meets this criterion; the basically psychotic individual does not. Kohut (1966, 1968, 1971, 1977) believes strongly that the narcissistic personality meets this criterion, although many disagree. Whether the borderline individual meets this criterion depends largely on one's criteria for the diagnosis of the borderline patient.

Psychoanalysis is basically designed for individuals with psychopathology at the neurotic structural level. These individuals include those with symptomatic neuroses but more frequently are people primarily with character (or personality) pathology. They usually suffer from chronic problems that, although far from disabling, interfere with their attaining their life goals, maximizing their potentials, and leading basically content lives. These individuals suffer from a wide assortment of character problems, including those of obsessive-compulsive, hysterical, depressive, masochistic, narcissistic, and mixed natures.

Although the character pathology varies markedly, these individuals commonly present themselves in one of several ways. One of the most common initial presentations is that of the individual who, although he does well on the job and has many friends, is unable to form sustaining, long-term, intimate personal relationships. Marriage is a goal, but something is stopping him from attaining this goal. This individual realizes that his problems are chronic, deep-seated, and lie within himself. Often he is somewhat sophisticated about psychoanalysis and specifically comes with that treatment modality in mind. This individual frequently, although not always, suffers from sexual difficulties, plus varying degrees of anxiety and depression, in addition to his presenting complaints. A second common initial presentation is that of the patient who, although she performs acceptably at work, feels that something is holding her back and stopping her from living up to her potential. There may be overt problems with her peers or boss, and there may be anxiety about succeeding. This person also has come to realize that her problems are chronic, deep-seated, and within herself. She may or may not additionally have problems in maintaining long-term, intimate relationships, and may or may not suffer accompanying anxiety or depression.

For individuals who have psychopathology at the neurotic structural level and who suffer from deep-seated character problems, most obviously manifested in failures in maintaining long-term intimate relationships or in failures in maximizing their potential at work, psychoanalysis is the treatment of choice. This is also the case for individuals with chronic symptomatic neuroses. For individuals who present clear-cut narcissistic problems, psychoanalysis, although recommended by some, remains controversial. Among individuals in the borderline group, psychoanalysis is generally considered only for a selected minority. Psychoanalysis is generally not considered for individuals at the psychotic structural level.

ANALYTICALLY ORIENTED PSYCHOTHERAPY

This chapter uses the terms *analytically oriented psychotherapy* and *dynamically oriented psychotherapy* to describe two different, yet somewhat related, types of therapy. The trappings of analytically oriented psychotherapy involve regularly scheduled sessions, usually two but sometimes three a week, held for varying periods of time. As in psychoanalysis, there is basically no contact between patient and psychotherapist outside of the appointments. Sessions are typically conducted with the patient and therapist sitting across from each other in comfortable chairs. The patient is usually told that the sessions are hers, that she can talk about whatever she chooses. In addition to discussing topics of her choice, the patient is encouraged to report seemingly extraneous thoughts and fantasies that occur to her during the sessions. As in psychoanalysis, areas of typical resistance to such discussion are often mentioned. Thus, the trappings of analytically oriented psychotherapy are both similar to and different from those of psychoanalysis.

Although the trappings are somewhat different, the therapist attempts to conduct analytically oriented psychotherapy in a manner as similar as possible to that of psychoanalysis. He tries to remain neutral, relies on clarifications and interpretations as much as possible, and tries to make maximum therapeutic use of the transference. Just as in psychoanalysis, he comments on resistances, tries to correlate the transference with current interactions and significant childhood relationships, and attempts to help the patient to understand gradually those aspects of herself about which she is unaware. This is analytically oriented psychotherapy in its pure form.

Even this pure form of analytically oriented psychotherapy is usually limited in effectiveness compared with psychoanalysis. With the patient constantly looking at the therapist, noting his expressions and mannerisms, she "learns" more about him than she would in psychoanalysis. She does not see him in as neutral a way and often has more difficulty "transferring" her feelings onto him. Without the use of the couch, without the process of free association, and with less frequent sessions, regression does not occur as easily, and the transference does not usually form with the same primitivity, intensity, or speed. The ability to form a regressed transference varies markedly from patient to patient. Even at its "best," however, with patients with psychopathology at the neurotic structural level, the quality of the transference in analytically oriented psychotherapy is rarely on a par with that in psychoanalysis. Although analytically oriented psychotherapy can be quite effective, it is the lack of a fully developed intense and regressed transference that limits this form of psychotherapy.

Many individuals undergoing analytically oriented psychotherapy are very similar to those undergoing psychoanalysis. Time and money limitations, fear of psychoanalysis *per se,* and lack of knowledge about the psychoanalytic process are the usual reasons that psychoanalysis proper is not chosen. Almost always these individuals would be better off in psychoanalysis. Sometimes these patients can start with psychoanalytically oriented psychotherapy, and then switch to psychoanalysis after resistances have decreased.

MODIFIED ANALYTICALLY ORIENTED PSYCHOTHERAPY

Modified analytically oriented psychotherapy involves the same trappings as analytically oriented psychotherapy. Modifications are in the areas that differentiate psychoanalysis from the other forms of psychotherapy: the analyst's neutrality, the development and resolution of the transference, and the emphasis on interpretation as the primary therapeutic intervention. Modifications are initiated because of the psychopathology of the patient, which makes unmodified analytically oriented psychotherapy difficult to impossible. Modified analytically oriented psychotherapy is ideally suited for many borderline individuals.

The area of least modification for borderline patients is the transference, which continues to be emphasized as the crucial forum through which the conflicts of the patient are resolved. This emphasis is especially suitable for borderline patients, because these individuals often form rapid, intense, and regressed transferences even without the use of the couch. It is the rapid mobilization of the transference that distinguishes the typical borderline patient from the typical neurotic. The latter becomes involved with the transference at a slower and more gradual pace, sometimes with difficulty. The neutrality of the analyst is maintained as much as possible, not so much regarding equidistance from id, ego, superego, and external reality, but in the sense of the therapist being nonjudgmental, noncritical, and totally focused on the patient, as elaborated in Chapter 15. Modifications regarding interventions vary greatly. In some borderline patients, there can be a preponderance of insight-oriented interventions; in others, the focus switches to supportive techniques.

With the ability of many borderline patients to regress easily and to become rapidly involved with the therapist and the transference, the opportunity to use analytically oriented psychotherapy is clear. However, because of the borderline individual's ego weaknesses and the propensity for too much regression, the modified approach is usually necessary.

DYNAMICALLY ORIENTED PSYCHOTHERAPY

The trappings of dynamically oriented psychotherapy involve regularly scheduled sessions, often one but sometimes two a week, held for varying periods of time. There is little contact between patient and psychotherapist outside of the appointments. Sessions are always conducted with the patient and therapist sitting across from each other. Basically the same instructions are given to the patient as in analytically oriented psychotherapy, although sometimes the instruction to report seemingly extraneous material is omitted.

The main difference between dynamically oriented psychotherapy and analytically oriented psychotherapy is the down-playing of the transference as a therapeutic modality in the former. Although transference reactions are noted, especially when they occur as resistances, the elaboration of the transference is not considered a major ingredient in this form of psychotherapy. Rather, the therapist and the patient focus much more exclusively on present-day interactions and relationships, and their correlation to the patient's past. Patient and therapist together try to understand the patient's present-day interactions on the basis of her sensitivities, vulnerabilities, and distortions, which originate in the past. A positive therapeutic alliance is fostered, and the therapist is sometimes mildly idealized. Occasional suggestion and education are employed, along with clarifications and partial interpretations, although the former techniques are by no means emphasized. Neutrality is maintained as much as possible.

Dynamically oriented psychotherapy is found particularly useful by some psychotherapists for a selected group of patients, often psychotic, but sometimes borderline, who present problems with the elaboration and working through of the transference. There is one group of borderline patients who start psychotherapy with a modified analytically oriented approach, and then after a reasonable therapeutic alliance has been established, switch to a dynamically oriented modality. Some psychotherapists routinely use dynamically oriented psychotherapy, both for patients who would benefit from a more analytically oriented approach and for those who would not.

Although dynamically oriented psychotherapy is listed

on the supportive end of the continuum, the degree of support varies in accordance with the therapist's choice of interventions. Thus, dynamically oriented psychotherapy can be utilized for neurotic individuals using mainly insight-oriented interventions. In contrast, it can be used for psychotic individuals, utilizing a preponderance of supportive techniques. Among psychoanalysts, there is debate about what type of psychotherapy is best for neurotic patients who are not in psychoanalysis. One group favors simulating analysis as much as possible. A second group, noting the difficulty in attaining transference regressions with neurotic patients in psychotherapy, favors using a dynamically oriented approach. Other therapists lean toward an analytically oriented modality for those neurotic patients (often hysterical in personality type) who can form somewhat of a regressed transference in psychotherapy, while employing a more dynamically oriented model for those neurotic patients (often obsessive in personality type) who have greater difficulty regressing.

SUPPORTIVE PSYCHOTHERAPY

In supportive psychotherapy, the patient comes for regularly scheduled sessions, usually once a week but sometimes more frequently, for varying but often lengthy periods. The principle underlying the number of sessions scheduled is virtually the opposite of that used in the more analytically oriented psychotherapies. In the latter approaches, increased sessions are used to promote intensity and regression. In supportive psychotherapy, the goal is to stop regression, not to promote it. Here more frequent sessions are employed to stem untoward regression, at times when the patient is having acute difficulty with some of his basic ego functions. When the patient is doing "well," a lower frequency of sessions, usually once a week, generally suffices. In supportive psychotherapy, contact between patient and therapist outside the sessions is promoted only to the extent that it is necessary to stem regression. Sessions are always conducted with the patient and therapist sitting across from each other. Instructions to the patient are simply to discuss those events in his life with which he is having difficulty.

Supportive psychotherapy is best suited for individuals with active disturbances in a number of their ego functions. This form of psychotherapy is indicated for a large group of basically psychotic individuals, although another large group of psychotic patients can benefit more from dynamically oriented psychotherapy, at least some of the time. Supportive psychotherapy is also used by some in the treatment of selected borderline individuals. This form of psychotherapy is sometimes supplemented by psychiatric medication.

The purpose of supportive psychotherapy is to help build up the patient's weak ego functions, hence the often-used term *ego building.* For this purpose many types of therapeutic intervention are employed, including education, suggestion, clarification, reassurance, advice, and instruction, but not usually interpretation. For these interventions to be most successful, the maintenance of a positive transference and a therapeutic alliance is exceptionally important. For this reason, the transference is usually not discussed unless it is a resistance. Likewise, transference distortions are often rapidly corrected by education and reality testing. In supportive psychotherapy the therapist is often unable to maintain a neutral position, although he should strive to do so when possible. For this kind of psychotherapy to proceed optimally, free association is not wanted. What is wanted is a detailed description of the day-to-day events that led to the patient's current difficulty with his ego functions. Hence, contrary to the more analytically oriented approaches, the focus is on the here and now, and reporting of weekly events is encouraged.

The initial goal of supportive psychotherapy is to help the patient strengthen and maintain his ego functioning so that he can adapt adequately in day-to-day interactions. When the patient begins to function acceptably in this realm, further goals are added. A second and more difficult goal is to help the patient identify and accept those areas in which he is sensitive and vulnerable to regression. Once these areas are identified and accepted by the patient, he can begin to learn to deal with them more effectively and gradually to respond to them by means other than regression. The tasks of helping the patient to identify these stressful areas and then to deal more effectively with them can be very time-consuming. As this work is pursued, the psychotherapeutic approach often becomes more exploratory and often switches to a dynamically oriented framework. If and when the patient is able to make this switch, it is considered a welcome psychotherapeutic advance.

Generally, individuals will maximize their gains in psychotherapy by undergoing the most insight-oriented approach that they can tolerate. Thus, if an individual clearly meets the criteria for psychoanalysis, he can expect to gain more from this approach than from analytically oriented psychotherapy. Likewise, if an individual can easily tolerate analytically oriented psychotherapy, he can expect to gain much more from that approach than from dynamically oriented psychotherapy. Analogously, a number of basically psychotic individuals can benefit more from dynamically oriented psychotherapy than from a more supportive approach, at least some of the time. If a patient is placed in a psychotherapy that he cannot tolerate, unnecessary regression can ensue. Careful evaluation in accordance with the ego-psychological diagnostic approach will usually enable the therapist to match the patient with the optimal therapeutic approach. In those cases in which, after thorough scrutiny, there is still uncertainty, a careful trial of the psychotherapy that seems most suitable can be undertaken. If the chosen form of psychotherapy does not prove to be optimal, it can always be modified or changed.

9

PSYCHOTHERAPY WITH THE BORDERLINE PATIENT

All five of the different types of psychotherapy reviewed in the last chapter have been used with some borderline patients. The treatment advocated reflects not only the therapist's theoretical persuasion and orientation, but also his definition of the term *borderline.* Thus, a number of psychoanalysts of the British school (Bion 1967, Rosenfeld 1965, Segal 1964) who employ psychoanalysis for basically psychotic individuals also use it for the borderline patient. Boyer (Boyer and Giovacchini 1967), Giovacchini (1984, 1993a,b), and Volkan (1987) recommend psychoanalysis with few modifications for borderline patients. Abend, Porder, and Willick (1983) write about classical psychoanalysis for relatively healthy borderline individuals. Analogously, psychoanalysis might make sense for some of the healthier subgroups of Meissner's classification (1984, 1988, 1993). Kernberg also allows for certain select borderline patients to be psychoanalyzed. At the other end of the continuum, Zetzel (1971) and Grinker (1975) use a purely supportive approach. Additionally, Rockland (1992) has recently contributed a volume on supportive psychotherapy for borderline patients.

The current consensus is on the use of modified analytically oriented psychotherapy. A number of these modified analytically oriented approaches have been described in the literature. These include the work of Kernberg (1968, 1975, 1978, 1980, 1982, Kernberg et al. 1989), Rinsley (1977, 1978, 1989), Masterson (1976, 1978, 1981), Adler and Buie (Adler 1981, 1985, 1993, Adler and Buie 1979, Buie and Adler 1982–1983), and Meissner (1988, 1993), among others. These approaches vary in detail, often in accordance with different underlying theoretical conceptualizations.

Gunderson (1984), Stone (1990b, 1993), and Chessick (1977, 1993) have also made useful contributions, offering more pragmatic emphases. Additionally, Waldinger and Gunderson (1987) have written a volume detailing psychotherapy with five borderline patients. Gunderson's approach is probably best classified as modified analytically oriented psychotherapy, whereas Stone and Chessick take a step in the direction of a dynamically oriented approach.

Of these approaches, Kernberg's is possibly the most influential today, followed closely by Adler's. Meissner has contributed an outstanding volume that includes basically everything one would want to know about psychotherapy with borderline patients. Because of the overwhelming influence and relevance of these three authors to my work, I have devoted separate short chapters to each of them. As an example of a more supportive but clearly reasonable and sound approach, I have chosen to devote a separate chapter to Rockland. In the remainder of this chapter, I discuss the work of Masterson and Rinsley; Giovacchini; Abend, Porder, and Willick; and Zetzel. At one time Masterson's writings were as well read as anyone's; possibly they still are. Together with Rinsley's, his ideas remain dominant and useful. Giovacchini is a creative and talented psychoanalyst, who presents his own intuitive brand of psychoanalysis with borderline patients. If anyone can analyze a borderline patient, it is Giovacchini. In contrast, Abend, Porder, and Willick try to do analyses with borderline patients in as classical a manner as possible. Zetzel presents an excellent example of a purely supportive approach.

MASTERSON AND RINSLEY

Masterson (1976, 1978) and Rinsley (1977, 1978) describe what they believe actually transpires in early childhood between the child and the parents to predispose the child to the borderline state. Although these authors later broadened their theory about etiology (Masterson 1981, Rinsley 1989), their ideas as described below relate well with their treatment approach. The mother, often a borderline individual herself and deriving much gratification from the symbiotic involvement with the child, withdraws her emotional availability when the child begins to make an effort to separate and individuate. This process peaks at the rapprochement subphase (16 to 25 months of age) of the separation-individuation period. Concomitant with the emotional withdrawal of the mother at this time is the absence and unavailability of the father. The child faces the dilemma of a rejecting, disapproving, and withdrawing (bad) mother if he strives for age-appropriate growth, or an approving, rewarding, and comforting mother if he remains passive and compliant. In response, the child internalizes what Masterson and Rinsley term *the split object relations unit.* This is composed of two part units, each consisting of three parts, as follows:

Withdrawing or Rejecting Part Unit

1. Representation of mother: attacking, critical, and withdrawing when child strives for age-appropriate growth
2. Representation of self: inadequate, helpless, bad
3. Affect: anger and frustration, covering depression related to abandonment by the mother

Rewarding Part Unit

1. Representation of mother: supportive and approving when child remains dependent, passive, and compliant
2. Representation of self: passive, compliant, good
3. Affect: feeling good, gratified

It is the persistence of this split object relations unit that leads to the psychopathology associated with the borderline patient.

The psychotherapeutic strategy of Rinsley and Masterson involves the activation, elaboration, and working through of the split object relations unit within the transference. The borderline patient starts therapy with the rewarding part unit being ego-syntonic and with little awareness of the psychological cost of this. The rewarding part unit is expressed in the general ego-syntonic borderline psychopathology, which came about because of the persistence of this part unit. From the outset the therapist begins a process of confrontation and clarification to demonstrate to the patient the self-destructive nature of this part unit. By this process the rewarding part unit becomes progressively ego-dystonic, and there is an activation of the withdrawing part unit. The withdrawing part unit, however, will be resisted, with the re-emergence of the rewarding part unit. A kind of circular process goes on, with continual confrontation and clarification of the destructiveness of the rewarding part unit, the emergence of the withdrawing part unit, resistance to this emergence, the re-emergence of the rewarding part unit, a repeat of the confrontation and clarification, and so forth.

With time, a new alliance between therapist and patient develops to help render the rewarding part unit ego-dystonic. This is an alliance, built up as the patient internalizes the therapist as a positive external object, between the therapist's healthy ego and the "embattled-reality ego" of the patient.

This alliance produces a new "healthy" object relations unit for the patient, as follows:

1. Representation of therapist: supportive and approving when patient strives for appropriate growth
2. Representation of self: capable, developing, good
3. Affect: feeling good, gratified

The activation of this new healthy object relations unit, in combination with the repetitive confrontations, clarifications, and later, interpretations involving the split object relations unit, allows the patient gradually to become aware of the part units within himself and work these through. Via the working-through process, the part units become integrated, and the healthy object relations unit becomes predominant. The working-through process includes efforts at understanding the childhood determinants of the split object relations unit and thus the cause of the psychopathology. The latter psychotherapeutic work is thought to include elements of "classical" analysis in an attempt to uncover unconscious childhood determinants.

This summary is an oversimplification of the technical aspects of the psychotherapeutic work of Masterson and Rinsley. The type of therapy is a modified analytically oriented approach. The therapist's neutrality is maintained, confrontation, clarification, and interpretation (later) are the primary therapeutic techniques, and the main therapeutic focus is on the exploration of the transference. Primitive transferences, based on all-good and all-bad object relations units, become immediately active in the treatment setting. It is the working through and resolution of these transferences that are the crucial aspects of the psychotherapy. With much psychotherapeutic work, the more primitive transferences are replaced by higher-level transferences. Thus, the psychotherapeutic process of Rinsley and Masterson, in broad outline, is similar to that of Kernberg. It differs from Kernberg's in its specificity. Kernberg (1982) considers Rinsley and Masterson to be describing work with what he calls infantile personalities, a subgroup of his borderline personality category.

GIOVACCHINI

Giovacchini (1984, 1993a,b) prefers the term *character disorder* to that of *borderline* (Goldstein 1994). He uses this term to describe any patient whose main psychopathology is expressed in terms of defects in psychic structure. Based on developmental level, he divides character disorders into several groups. The most primitive of these are the schizoid states. These patients have their difficulties originating in the earliest months of life, at a time Giovacchini calls the prementational phase, where core difficulties are at a prepsychological level. Giovacchini conceptualizes these patients as having a psyche without intermediary links, without bridges or connections between lower and upper levels of the psychic apparatus. Empty spaces in the psyche are somatically organized and devoid of psychological content. Symptoms of these patients are often expressed as psychosomatic disorders. These patients use schizoid withdrawal as their main adaptation, and often feel lacking or dead.

Borderline states are a little less primitive than the schizoid personalities. These patients move toward the world rather than away, but they do it in an awkward and inept way. They are deficient in technique and knowledge, and are lacking in basic structure and self-esteem. A little less primitive are the character neuroses. These patients have a repertoire of adaptive defensive techniques and often adjust adequately on a superficial level. However, they respond to stress either by anxiety and feelings of inadequacy or by narcissistic defenses. They often use externalization to create a world similar to their childhood environments.

All of these patients fit into the borderline spectrum as commonly defined today. They present with fragmented personalities and defective self representations, and have problems adapting to the external world and establishing reasonable interpersonal relationships. They are basically concrete and mechanistic in their thinking and display structural defects and discontinuities. They often come from very traumatic backgrounds and frequently react to the traumas by encapsulating them and splitting them off from their main psychic contents.

Giovacchini writes about psychoanalysis with these extremely troubled patients. The psychoanalysis he describes is very different from that with neurotic patients, yet is probably as close to that process as possible, given his patient population. Emphasis is on the establishment of a holding environment, where the patient can regress without disruptive acting out. Within this setting the aim of therapy is toward the acquisition of psychic structure and the gaining of further cohesion of the psychic apparatus, rather than the resolution of intrapsychic conflict. The analytic relationship recapitulates the early developmental phase, and the holding environment provides what was destructively lacking in that phase. The analyst must be totally flexible and totally nonintrusive. There can be no basic rule, because this can be reminiscent of early assaults. Giovacchini talks of doing therapy in a transitional space, where grim reality can be converted to playful fantasy. In the transitional space, the patient can develop the capacities for flexibility, allusion, and psychological-mindedness.

Giovacchini describes analytic situations that unwittingly replicate aspects of the early traumatic environment, something he calls the psychoanalytic paradox. Some patients, most comfortable with environments similar to their early childhood, contribute to this by projecting destructive and abandoning introjects onto the therapist and by externalizing the infantile environment onto the office. The analyst's response to this is to create a holding environment devoid of noxious elements of the past.

Giovacchini elaborates on the type of interpretations that are most effective with patients in the borderline group. He does not advocate traditional interpretations of the type made to neurotic patients. Instead he recommends starting with what he calls phenomenological interpretations, or interpretations that refer to external qualities of the self, such as mannerisms, appearance, and attitudes. He also advocates linking interpretations, or ones that link outside events with internal processes. Nontransference interpretations are also often useful, particularly with narcissistic patients who become upset with too much emphasis on the analyst. These three types of interpretations, all helping the patient to deal with aspects of himself about which he was previously unaware, are easily accepted by the borderline patient.

Although Giovacchini utilizes a theoretical framework that is somewhat idiosyncratic, his thinking is certainly compatible with other authors. Many of his ideas are imaginative, stimulating, and ultimately very useful for the group of clearly disturbed patients about whom he writes. There is no doubt that the patients that Giovacchini writes about are in the borderline spectrum, most frequently at the lower end. Giovacchini (1993a) also writes about analytically oriented psychotherapy with a similar group of patients. It is unclear when he chooses psychoanalysis versus analytically oriented psychotherapy.

ABEND, PORDER, AND WILLICK

Abend, Porder, and Willick (1983) discussed the concept of the borderline patient with about twenty-five of their colleagues over a 4-year period. Based on a compilation of "noncontroversial phenomenological" items taken from a review of the literature of Deutsch (1942), Knight (1953), Gitelson (1958), Frosch (1964), Stone (1954), and Kernberg (1966, 1967), they formulated a list of descriptive features of borderline patients, as follows:

1. The pathology tends to invade the entire character structure and to be relatively stable.
2. Although the relationship to reality is impaired, as evidenced in perceptual distortions, poor judgment, and states of disturbed sense of reality, there remains either rapid reversibility of the defects or the persistent intactness of some degree of reality testing.
3. Interpersonal relations are infantile, with egocentricity, demandingness, and exploitiveness, and sometimes with passivity, overidealization, and submissiveness.
4. The life history is likely to reveal evidence of severe impairment.
5. Polysymptomatic clinical pictures, covering almost the entire range of neurotic symptomatology, are presented.
6. There may be psychotic fragments, primitive wishes and fantasies, and primary process thinking.
7. Narcissistic features are emphasized by many theorists.
8. Atypical, intense, early transference reactions occur. These are characterized by unusually strong affects and contradictory, unintegrated attitudes toward the analyst, and an inability to understand the unrealistic feelings and attitudes toward the analyst.
9. The prominence of aggressive conflicts is noted by some.
10. There is substantial disturbance in the area of affect, characterized by inappropriate, labile, absent, false, overintense, and poorly controlled emotion.

11. Specific and characteristic countertransference reactions are evoked.

Four patients satisfying these descriptive features, all having completed what the authors thought were classical psychoanalyses, were studied in detail. Based on this study, Abend, Porder, and Willick concluded that psychoanalysis is indicated for at least some borderline patients. The psychoanalyses of the four patients studied, although similar to classical psychoanalyses, were in some ways different from that of the usual neurotic. In particular, there was the need to interpret and reinterpret projective mechanisms carefully. There was the need to pay close attention to partial failures in reality testing. Sadomasochistic conflicts, acting out, and the pervasiveness of transference distortions demanded special attention. Change took place very slowly and intermittently, and discouragement within the analysts was frequent.

Abend and co-workers expressed disagreement with Kernberg, Rinsley, Masterson, and others in certain areas. They saw little value in confronting the patient's contradictory attitudes during assessment interviews. They disagreed with the selective focus on the negative transference, and took issue with emphasizing aggressive over libidinal conflicts. They disagreed with the suggestion of avoiding genetic interpretations early in the treatment, believing that these interpretations, when possible, were helpful. They found the material forthcoming in the opening phases of treatment to be extremely confusing and obscure, and were unable to see the primitive transferences described by others until much later in the treatment. They did not conceptualize the conflicts that emerged in treatment as coming from specific developmental times, such as the rapprochement subphase of the separation-individuation period; instead, they were impressed by the extent to which the material of their patients reflected concerns from various developmental periods. They did not advocate understanding and interpreting material in any preplanned manner. Instead, their basic therapeutic approach was similar to that used with healthier patients. No special techniques were thought to be needed or recommended.

Careful scrutiny (Goldstein 1985, Gunderson 1984, Waldinger and Gunderson 1987) of the four patients reveals that they are healthier than the more disturbed group of individuals to whom the term *borderline* is usually applied. If one thinks in terms of a borderline spectrum, these patients would clearly fall at the healthy end. Despite this, the successful analyses of these individuals is noteworthy in itself. Yet one needs to be cautioned not to generalize the findings from these healthier borderline patients to the larger group of patients carrying the borderline diagnosis.

ZETZEL

Zetzel (1971) believes that there are three developmental steps in the attainment of definitive psychic structure, all initiated in the early mother–child relationship. The first is the achievement of definitive self–object differentiation. The second is the capacity to recognize, tolerate, and master separation, loss, and narcissistic injury. The third is the internalization of an ego identification and self-esteem that will permit autonomy and the capacity to maintain stable one-to-one relationships. The borderline individual displays some difficulty with all three steps. There is only a relative failure in achieving the first step, most often expressed under stress and usually readily reversible. Regarding the second step, there is again a relative but this time a more significant failure, but one that can be considerably alleviated with psychotherapy. The borderline individual has only limited capabilities for achieving the third step, and for this reason, many such patients are relatively interminable in psychotherapy.

Zetzel believes that intensive psychotherapy can present

dangers to patients who suffer from these developmental failures. She holds that these patients tend to regress too much during intensive psychotherapy, tend to blur reality and transference, and are intolerant of painful affects associated with regressive transferences. Therefore, regressions are to be avoided; focus instead should be on progression and mastery. Zetzel's psychotherapeutic technique is based on the necessity for developing and maintaining a stable, realistic, and consistent patient–therapist relationship. She posits that regular but limited contact (seldom more than once a week) is optimal in maintaining a good working relationship. Improvement is best achieved by the establishment of a new and better relationship than had been attained during early development, a relationship based on a working alliance and involving minimal transference. During psychotherapy meetings, considerable activity and structure are used to focus actively on the patient's problems. Zetzel believes that this type of psychotherapy can help certain borderline patients maintain a high degree of adaptation, as long as the therapist remains available to the patient for an unlimited period of time.

Zetzel's type of psychotherapy is clearly a supportive approach. Although it does enable the borderline patient to correct some of his deficiencies, it accepts other deficits as givens and tries to help the patient to adapt to his limitations as well as possible.

10

KERNBERG

Kernberg (1967, 1975, 1976, 1980, 1984) with his colleagues (1989) has provided a systematized approach to psychoanalytic psychotherapy with the borderline patient. "Expressive psychotherapy," as he calls it, fits into the model of modified analytically oriented psychotherapy. Compared to other approaches Kernberg keeps his modifications to a minimum. He views the borderline individual's core problem as the difficulty in integrating good and bad self representations and object representations. The patient actively uses splitting and other related primitive defenses, has not attained libidinal object constancy, and does not have a consolidated integrated identity. The goal of expressive psychotherapy is to convert splitting and related primitive defenses to higher-level defenses, and to enhance the patient's ability to experience himself and others as coherent, integrated, and realistically perceived individuals.

Kernberg's expressive psychotherapy focuses on the transference. By a continual process of clarifying and interpreting good and bad self and object representations as they enter into the transference, the therapist helps the patient integrate these varying representations into whole objects having both good and bad characteristics. Eventually, the patient attains a more differentiated view of himself and others. It must be noted that this is not an easy process. Primitive transferences are rapidly mobilized and can be quite chaotic and confusing. The therapist must learn to tolerate this confusion, identify the transferences, discuss the identified transferences with the patient, note the patient's response to the discussion, and interpret the defenses within the transference.

Kernberg emphasizes establishing a contract at the onset of therapy. Initial instructions to the patient stress the patient's responsibilities in the therapy, including the need for honest communication and for keeping the therapist informed about life events. When there are no pressing problems in the patient's life, he should use the sessions to express freely whatever comes to mind. These initial instructions are used as a way of structuring the therapy, as something to return to whenever the patient deviates from the task. When the history indicates problems involving destructive acting out, these need to be addressed at the time of contract setting. Discussion includes the likelihood of acting out during the treatment and the establishment of a plan of action if this does occur.

In the course of therapy, any violations of the contract are rapidly addressed. Confrontation and interpretation are the preferred techniques, but when these are not possible, limit-setting is invoked. Limits that are less restrictive should always be initiated before ones that are more restrictive. While the contract is being set, resistances to it should be addressed by realistic reasoning. It is only after the contract is established that interpretation is utilized.

In conducting a session, Kernberg recommends initial focus on issues having the most significant affect. He includes issues where there is an inappropriate or striking lack of affect. Transference is always emphasized, but if the most significant affect involves items outside the transference, this latter has priority. Items that are overly destructive take priority over everything else. These include suicide or homicide threats, overt threats to the continuation of the treatment, dishonesty, and contract breeches, in that order of importance.

Regarding interpretation, the dominant material (that with the most affect or inappropriate lack of it) should be addressed first. Material should be approached from surface downward, with material closest to consciousness addressed first. Interpretations should describe the patient as being in conflict, with defense being interpreted before that which is defended against. The patient's motivation for his defensive position should be included in the interpretation. Interpretations should only be made when the therapist is relatively certain that his hypothesis will contribute to further understanding and when the patient is unlikely to arrive easily at the hypothesis himself. Interpretations are never made unless there is agreement between patient and therapist about the reality of what is being addressed. It is advisable not to make interpretations, nor to bring up new material near the end of the session.

Kernberg goes into detail regarding what he calls the early phase of treatment. In this phase the therapist is always listening to the material with the goal of identifying self and object representations. Kernberg outlines five steps in the process of identification and interpretation of these self and object representations. Step 1 involves experiencing and tolerating the confusion that ensues in the therapist's mind as he tries to sort out the rapidly changing self and object images. Step 2 involves identifying the representations and conceptualizing them in a way that can be easily explained to the patient. Step 3 involves naming the representations for the patient. The therapist tries to do this at a time when the patient is curious about the nature of the interaction with the therapist. He tries to characterize the process as specifically as possible, correlating each self representation with its corresponding object representation and with its linking affect. It should be noted that there are rapid changes from one representation to another and the process of identifying and naming can be quite difficult. Step 4 involves careful attention to the patient's response to the naming. Responses to correct naming can lead to the self–object interaction named becoming more pronounced, to a sudden interchange of the self image with the object image (via projection and introjection), to evidence of insight by the patient, or to blanket denial. Incorrect naming can lead to overt disagreement, blanket denial, or acknowledged agreement in an effort to please the therapist. Step 5 involves interpreting the primitive defenses that are used to separate the self and object images. This includes a demonstration of how the defenses minimize anxiety.

In this so-called early phase of treatment, negative transferences are focused on and interpreted as fully as possible. Regarding positive transferences, those involving grossly exaggerated primitive idealizations need to be rapidly interpreted, while more modulated aspects of the positive transference are left alone. Because the patient often distorts the therapist's interpretations, examination of how the patient receives and processes any interpretation needs exploration. Genetic material is avoided, because it can lead to confusion between transference and reality.

The basic techniques of expressive psychotherapy are the same as those of psychoanalysis: analysis of the transference, interpretation, and technical neutrality. Unlike psychoanalysis, however, the analysis of the transference is consistently correlated with the here and now, in the hope that the therapy does not become isolated from the rest of the patient's life. Clarifications, confrontations, and interpretations are utilized as much as possible, with other therapeutic techniques discouraged. Regressive tendencies in the borderline patient, however, can lead to severe acting out and psychotic distortions within the transference. Here a switch in therapeutic technique is required, and technical neutrality cannot be totally maintained. Interventions involving limit-setting and the structuring of the external life of the patient, sometimes with time-limited hospitalizations, may become necessary. When this happens, a return to technical neutrality with a re-emphasis on interpretation should follow as soon as possible.

As the early phase nears completion, the more primitive transferences are worked through and replaced by more typically neurotic transferences. The patient is then better able to integrate self and object representations of varying affects. The role of the therapist now is to help the patient tolerate his newly acquired ambivalent feelings. As this ambivalence is tolerated, the patient can see himself and others as more complex people with depth and self-reflection. The advanced phase of treatment becomes more and more similar to work with predominantly neurotic individuals. Genetic interpretations begin to play a role, free association is encouraged, and dream work is increasingly utilized. Termination should be considered when the treatment has reached the point of diminishing returns. A termination date 6 months in advance is recommended, and the termination phase often resembles that of the neurotic individual. There should not be a reduction in sessions in the termination phase.

CRITIQUE

With the focus on the analysis of the transference, interpretation as the primary therapeutic technique, and the maintenance of technical neutrality, Kernberg's expressive psychotherapy clearly fits into the category of analytically oriented psychotherapy. Although modifications are utilized as little as possible, this therapy still fits into the category of modified analytically oriented psychotherapy. This approach is as systematized and as clearly delineated as any in the literature. Basically all the therapeutic recommendations are well thought out, nicely elaborated, and reasonable.

The idea of spelling out basic instructions and establishing a contract at the beginning of the therapy is clearly useful. This provides a basic framework, to be referred back to during the course of therapy. In my experience, however, many regressed borderline patients are not initially able to collaborate with a contract in an authentic way. If this is the case, I suggest bypassing or minimizing the contract at the beginning, and returning to it later in the treatment. This is elaborated in Chapter 16.

The main problem in doing Kernberg's expressive psychotherapy is the detailed focus on the self and object representations and their linking affects as they enter into the transference. To do this well, one needs to be an expert in the type of object relations theory that Kernberg uses. Most therapists are not such experts. One possibility is to follow Kernberg's suggestions but to substitute a more ego-psychological model (or another alternative) for Kernberg's object relations approach.

11

ADLER

Adler (1985, 1993, Adler and Buie 1979; Buie and Adler 1982–1983) details and elaborates his definitive approach to psychotherapy with the borderline patient. Drawing on his theoretical model emphasizing the relative deficiency of holding introjects as the core problem of the borderline patient, as described in Chapter 3, Adler divides his treatment into three phases. Phase I is the phase most relevant to borderline patients and thus will be emphasized here.

First, several key concepts will be discussed. Adler uses the term *aloneness* to describe a very uncomfortable feeling state that occurs in a person with a tenuous capacity to maintain holding introjects, when that person is faced with the perceived loss of a holding selfobject. This feeling, somewhat akin to emptiness, occurs in the borderline patient after he has become attached to his therapist, when threatened by various separations (such as vacations, the end of sessions, etc.). At times, aloneness can intensify to feelings of panic; at its worst, it can be related to fears of annihilation of the self. When a patient feels that his therapist is unable to assuage his aloneness, he can become enraged. Direct rage can be supplemented by the projection of hostile introjects and by feelings of envy.

Adler uses the term *primitive guilt* to describe guilt that is easily projected and has an all-or-none quality. It is related to the intensity of the borderline patient's hatred, sometimes of himself, sometimes projected with the idea that others hate him. Because of this primitive guilt, the patient can feel undeserving of the therapist's help, leading to rejection of the therapist's efforts.

The *need–fear dilemma* refers to the intense need for and the equally intense fear of others. The need relates to the regressed borderline patient's use of incorporation and fusion as a means of combatting aloneness. The fear is regressively expressed as the fear of a loss of self and object representations, although this actual loss rarely occurs. The understanding of the borderline patient's aloneness, primitive guilt, and need–fear dilemma is integral to beginning psychotherapy with Adler's model.

The goal of Phase I of the psychotherapy is to establish and maintain a relationship in which the therapist can be used as a holding selfobject. When this goal is attained, the patient is able to develop insight into the nature of his aloneness, to acquire a solid evocative memory of the therapist, and to form adequate holding introjects. This process would occur naturally over time, except for a number of psychodynamic obstacles that block it. These obstacles are related to the occurrence of aloneness in the therapeutic relationship, to the need–fear dilemma, and to the emergence of primitive guilt. It is the very stormy process of working through these psychodynamic obstacles in the transference that characterizes Phase I of the therapy. This process is accomplished by repetitive clarifications, confrontations, and interpretations.

Although the approach in Phase I is mainly insight-oriented, the treatment must be conducted in a supportive way, to help maintain the evolving tenuous introjects and to help prevent the feeling of aloneness to regress to annihilation anxiety. The therapist must do everything possible to act as a holding selfobject in reality. Techniques to sustain this role, such as extra appointments, telephone calls, the use of transitional objects, and rigorous clarifications of the reality of the therapist as a holding object, must be brought into play. If regression is severe, brief hospitalizations may be required. The essence of the treatment is an interpretative approach in a holding environment. Over time the patient learns that the therapist is an enduring, reliable, and good holding selfobject. Via the process of working through, with insight and internalization, the patient is able to convert the holding selfobject into holding introjects.

Phase I ends when the holding introjects are fairly firmly established. This, in essence, is the end of the core borderline issues. The problem now is that the holding introjects are unrealistic and highly idealized, patterned after qualities of whatever positive introjects were formed in the early years. The aim of Phase II is to convert these unrealistic idealized holding introjects into more realistic mature holding introjects. Adler models his work after that of Kohut in this phase. By a process of "optimal disillusionment," in which the patient gradually notices differences between the idealized holding introjects and the actual holding qualities of the therapist, work in this phase takes place with little direct therapeutic intervention. Ultimately the holding introjects are modified in accordance with reality.

Because most of Adler's borderline patients also exhibit serious narcissistic pathology, Phase II addresses these problems as well. As the idealized holding introjects are modified in accordance with reality, so also are the narcissistic introjects. As Phase II evolves, the borderline patient begins to look much like the narcissistic patient of Kohut; accordingly, psychotherapeutic work proceeds in accordance with Kohut's recommendations. Adler believes that work with the pathological narcissism cannot be undertaken until the holding introjects are adequately stable. Thus, Phase II must be relatively advanced in this regard before definitive work with the narcissism can take place.

The aim of Phase III is to convert the holding introjects into more definitive psychic structures. By the end of this phase, a rather mature ego and superego are established. Specifically, the ego has the capacity for pleasurable confidence in the self and for directing affectionate love toward the self. Correspondingly, the superego is no longer harsh and now serves as a source of a realistically deserved sense of worth. The work of Phase III continues along the lines of Kohut's conceptualizations; a form of internalization, termed the *transmuting internalization* by Kohut, plays a major role. Various kinds of subtle selfobject functions continue to be necessary to provide the experiences out of which the patient can, via identification, develop his own autonomous capacities. These capacities include the ability to be held and soothed on one's own, the feeling of the reality of one's own self-worth and competence, and the ability to be affectionately loving to oneself. At the end of this phase, the patient has acquired genuine psychological stability, varying in degree from patient to patient.

CRITIQUE

Adler believes that the important elements of his psychotherapeutic approach are psychoanalytic. Basically, the therapist's neutrality is maintained, confrontation, clarification, and interpretation are the primary therapeutic techniques, and the main therapeutic focus is on the exploration of the transference. Techniques involving the use of the therapist as a selfobject are required however, and the reliance on these techniques makes this form of psychotherapy more supportive. Nevertheless, Adler's approach qualifies as a form of modified analytically oriented psychotherapy.

The focus on the deficiency of holding introjects, unique

to this form of psychotherapy, is of clear clinical value. The unfolding of Phase I, with the emergence of the psychodynamic obstacles that characterize it, is applicable to many borderline patients. The correlation of this psychotherapy with a solid underlying theoretical base, even though the theory can be a bit cumbersome at times, enhances the therapeutic work. The view that borderline patients in Phase II become very similar to Kohut's narcissistic personalities and do best with psychotherapeutic techniques advocated by Kohut is more questionable.

12

MEISSNER

Meissner (1982–1983, 1983, 1984, 1988, 1993) feels that borderline patients are best thought of as a heterogeneous group of individuals, represented by a spectrum of levels and degrees of pathological personality functioning. Thus, when he suggests psychotherapeutic strategy and technique, he is always aware of the variations on the spectrum. He typically suggests one set of techniques for patients at the lower end of the spectrum and another for patients at the upper end.

Meissner emphasizes the establishment of the therapeutic alliance as the cornerstone of doing psychotherapy with borderline patients. He notes the difficulty in establishing such an alliance and the need for continuous attention to alliance factors throughout the psychotherapy. He considers contractual arrangements, the logistics of therapy, and some initial agreement and understanding of the roles of therapist and patient as factors that strengthen the therapeutic alliance. A consistent attitude of the therapist, insisting on the patient's meaningful involvement in the therapeutic process, is also desirable. Limiting destructive acting out and dealing with early transference distortions likewise contribute to the establishment of the alliance. It is of utmost importance to try to develop a relationship with the patient that is trustworthy, reliable, responsible, honest, and consistent. The basic structure of the therapeutic situation needs to be maintained, but this must be done in a holding environment. The holding posture is emphasized more in patients at the lower end of the borderline spectrum, while the structuring posture is emphasized in patients at the higher end of the spectrum.

Meissner maintains that alliance problems often remain a problem with borderline patients throughout the course of therapy. In patients at the lower end of the spectrum, impediments to the therapeutic alliance often take the form of acute disruptions such as various forms of acting out and self-destructive behavior with acute regressions. In patients at the higher end, the difficulties in the therapeutic alliance are more subtle, often occurring gradually over time, and usually taking the form of various distortions of the alliance and misalliances. When a disruption in the alliance occurs, repair of the therapeutic alliance takes precedence over everything else.

Regarding the transference, it should be allowed to develop as much as possible without intervention. Interventions are necessary when the transference creates a resistance to the treatment process or when it becomes sufficiently disruptive as to undermine the therapeutic alliance. Priority is always given to maintaining the therapeutic alliance, as interpretation of the transference can only be done effectively where there is a positive alliance.

When interpreting, the tone, style, and manner of the interpretation are emphasized. An empathic atmosphere is helpful so that the patient will gradually be able to internalize the therapist as an accepting, reasonable person. Meissner focuses on what he calls *affirmative interpretations,* as elaborated by Schaffer (1986). An affirmative interpretation is made in such a way that it is experienced as empathic and respectful. This type of interpretation is usually well received, because it shows an appreciation for the difficulties the patient is experiencing.

Meissner makes the important distinction between displacement transferences and projective transferences, noting the dominance of the former in neurotic patients and higher-level borderline patients, and the dominance of the latter in lower-level borderline patients. Sometimes the projective transferences can take the form of externalizations, where the current environment is seen and reshaped in accordance with aspects of the borderline patient's early life.

Meissner conceptualizes both displacement and projective transferences in terms of introjective configurations. He views borderline patients as maintaining several different and contradictory introjective configurations, often shifting in accordance with the dynamics of the psychotherapy. These configurations occur in two sets: the victim–aggressor introjects and the introjects of grandiosity and inferiority.

The transference often goes back and forth between victim and aggressor introjects, on the one hand, and inferior and superior introjects, on the other hand. This is particularly characteristic of the lower end of the spectrum, where these introjective configurations remain close to the surface. In the higher end of the spectrum, the introjective configurations are more stable and less easily projected. Here the patient often stabilizes himself around one configuration, with the complementary configuration ready for activation under regression.

In dealing with the introjective configurations, Meissner recommends a process somewhat analogous to that of Kernberg regarding self and object representations. Identifying and exploring the configurations take place before more definitive interpretation. Introjects of inferiority are more available for interpretation than introjects of superiority. A useful method is for the therapist to ally himself with the inferior introject, understanding and accepting this position in an empathic way. Only later is there focus on the introject of superiority. The same might be said for interpreting the victim introject before the aggressor introject, again in the same affirmative manner. With time, the victim and aggressor introjects need to be understood as a complementary pair, and likewise the introjects of inferiority and superiority.

Interpretation is always preceded by a process of clarification and confrontation. At the lower end of the spectrum these latter techniques play a much larger role than interpretations *per se.* At the upper end of the spectrum, by contrast, the process of interpretation can resemble that with a neurotic patient. Regarding genetic material, Meissner believes that direct interpretation can be useful, but usually at the upper end of the spectrum where displacement transferences dominate.

Limit-setting often is needed to curtail acting out and regressive behaviors. In lower-level patients, this can be seen as a caring intervention. In higher-level patients, limits take a more subtle form, of sharing concern and exploring consequences of possible courses of action. In these patients, the emphasis is much less on limits and more on other techniques. Limits are not used if clarifications, confrontations, and interpretations can be effective in forestalling acting out.

As might be expected, Meissner recommends various forms of psychotherapy, depending on the individual borderline patient. In general, he advocates a somewhat supportive and empathic approach, although certainly dynamically oriented, for lower-level borderline patients. The need for flexibility on the part of the therapist cannot be overemphasized here. For higher-level borderline patients, he recommends a more exploratory and insight-oriented approach. With some higher-level patients, he recommends psychoanalysis, although he states that the psychoanalysis here might not be greatly different from analytically oriented psychotherapy.

CRITIQUE

Because Meissner writes so extensively about therapeutic technique and intervention, the above presentation only provides highlights. Meissner views the three legs of the therapeutic tripod in the treatment of the borderline patient to be the therapeutic alliance, the transference, and the countertransference. His ideas about the countertransference have been largely omitted because they correspond directly to his ideas about the alliance and the transference.

It is difficult to disagree with any of Meissner's recommendations; they are all sound, thoughtful, and useful. I find his distinction between displacement and projective transferences, his focus on the two complementary introjective configurations (victim and aggressor introjects and introjects of inferiority and superiority), and his concept of affirmative interpretation greatly relevant. Likewise his comparison and contrast of techniques for patients at the lower end of the spectrum with those for patients at the upper end are highly practical. With this in mind, one gains perspective when he notes that the early activation of chaotic transferences occurs only at the lower end of the spectrum. Meissner's focus on the therapeutic alliance and its relationship to the transference is central for work with borderline patients.

13

ROCKLAND

Rockland (1992) has recently published a book on supportive psychotherapy with the borderline patient. Relying on his previous book (1989) on supportive therapy in general, he sets forth and elaborates the principles and guidelines of this type of psychotherapy. Using psychodynamic and psychoanalytic principles, he names his therapy *psychodynamically oriented supportive therapy*. The goals of this kind of therapy are the return to homeostasis for patients in crisis and the strengthening of ego functions with subsequent improved adaptation. In this therapy, the therapist tends to be more verbally active and less frustrating. The development and elaboration of the transference are discouraged, and the real relationship is emphasized.

Negative transferences are rapidly addressed, with discrepancies between the transference and reality rapidly noted. Sometimes transferences are deflected to significant others in the patient's current life. Strict limits are used for acting out of the negative transferences or for rageful transferences. The therapist might even end the session early if necessary, to help the patient maintain behavioral control. Regarding positive transferences, the strategy is to encourage a mildly positive transference, while addressing overidealized and overeroticized transferences in an analogous manner to negative transferences. The mildly positive transference is used to help form a therapeutic alliance, through which the process of identification can occur. The therapeutic alliance, although crucial, is very difficult to develop and establish. If it does develop, it often is not until the late phases of treatment. Because the rules for therapeutic interventions are less clear in supportive than exploratory psychotherapy, countertransference acting out is a constant danger. Thus, countertransference needs to be watched and monitored more closely than in more exploratory work.

In supportive therapy there is a focus on conscious and preconscious material with an avoidance of the unconscious. Basically all techniques except interpretation are used. These include encouraging the therapeutic alliance, furnishing hope and reassurance, giving suggestion and advice, educating the patient, accepting abreaction (without interpretation), making environmental interventions, reframing, giving encouragement and praise, emphasizing strengths and talents, prescribing medication, making clarifications and confrontations, and furnishing a model for identification. Reframing means helping the patient to view the situation in more realistic terms.

In addition to the above techniques, thought by Rockland to require little psychodynamic sophistication, there are other strategies that are more complex. These include strengthening adaptive defenses while undermining maladaptive ones, supplying inexact interpretations, helping the patient use benign projections and introjections, and using psychodynamic understanding of the patient to help determine the nature of the intervention.

All of the above interventions are used to help strengthen the different ego functions, to help decrease pressure from the drives, and to help undermine harsh superego demands. Defenses and resistances are evaluated according to their adaptive/maladaptive values. Basically adaptive defenses are encouraged, whereas maladaptive ones are confronted and undermined. Regression is never desired; with this in mind, logical thought is encouraged, while free association is discouraged.

The first phase of supportive psychotherapy, the diagnostic evaluation and treatment planning, includes four tasks: clinical evaluation, diagnostic formulation, treatment planning, and contract setting. All of these tasks are openly discussed, with much feedback from therapist to patient. Particular emphasis is given to the contract setting. The purpose here is to set up a structure that will safeguard the treatment from future attempts at undermining. Here a prediction is made as to what behavior patterns might occur to later threaten the treatment. These are identified and discussed, with decisions about how they will be handled built into the contract. Thus, the contract includes a set of agreements that can be referred back to whenever there are resistances and threats to the treatment. Here joint collaboration between patient and therapist is strongly emphasized.

The early phase of treatment shortly ensues and also includes four tasks: educating the patient about the treatment, setting goals for the treatment, structuring and strengthening the therapeutic alliance, and identifying both the main maladaptive behavior and defenses to be undermined and the main strengths and adaptive behavior to be supported. Goals, including focus on strengthening of the various ego functions, need to be simple, realistic, and mutually agreed upon.

The middle phase of treatment consists of the working through of the major issues already identified, plus a focus on and working through of any new issues. Here there is repetitive focus on maladaptive defenses and on marked transference distortions, with the therapist consistently confronting negative patterns both within and without the transference. At the same time, positive changes are encouraged and praised. Time is needed for the process of identification with the therapist to occur.

Termination begins with the setting of a termination date. This phase is much less definitive than in more exploratory approaches. Various resistances and acting out are reasonably accepted. Stopping before the agreed upon date or decreasing the frequency of sessions by the patient's request are permissible. Upon termination, the therapist always communicates his availability in the future at time of need, either for occasional sessions or for further psychotherapy.

Rockland notes that, in actuality, almost all therapy with borderline patients involves mixtures of supportive and exploratory interventions. He also notes that some borderline patients can benefit best from a mostly insight-oriented approach. However, he is clear that the vast majority of borderline patients benefit best from primarily supportive therapy. In fact, he states that at least 75 percent of the patients who meet the *DSM-III-R* criteria for borderline personality disorder should be treated, at least initially, with a primarily supportive approach.

Regarding the choice of exploratory versus supportive work, Rockland feels that exploratory work should be considered when the patient displays a number of positive qualities, such as high intelligence, likability, psychological-mindedness, good motivation, and relatively decent ego functioning. Those patients meeting only five of the eight *DSM-III-R* criteria for borderline personality disorder are included in this group. Patients with prominent problems in identity, with less significant problems in impulsivity and affective instability, are also considered here, as are patients who overlap with diagnoses of narcissistic, dependent, and obsessional personalities. Rockland adds that there are a number of patients who start with a supportive approach, who can later be switched to a more exploratory method.

CRITIQUE

Utilizing a model based on psychodynamic understanding, Rockland outlines a very reasonable and useful form of psychotherapy. I basically agree with most of Rockland's suggested techniques. Most borderline patients do benefit from and need a number of the more supportive elements advocated by Rockland. My main disagreement with Rockland is in the downplaying of the transference. In my experience, the transference needs to be emphasized with the majority of borderline patients. Often there is no choice; the transference simply hits you in the face, sooner or later and usually sooner. Thus, I am more inclined to accept Rockland's suggestions in a therapeutic context where the transference plays a more dominant role.

Another disagreement is with Rockland's emphasis on the contract. As I have said previously, contract setting cannot be authentically accomplished early in the treatment with many borderline patients. Thus, although I agree with the suitability of a contract, I feel that its establishment must often wait until later in the treatment. I also have reservations about early discussion of the patient's dynamics. Not only is the patient often unable to process such information at an early stage, but it often takes the therapist a prolonged period of time to reasonably understand and formulate the dynamics himself.

The choice of insight-oriented therapy versus more supportive therapy is often dictated by the patient. It is sometimes a question of an approach with mainly supportive elements or no approach at all. With this in mind, Rockland's idea that 75 percent of borderline patients need a more supportive approach, at least initially, if anything, seems to be an understatement. With the above qualifiers, Rockland offers an abundance of excellent and relevant strategies and techniques for working with borderline patients.

Part III

TECHNIQUE

14

BASIC STRATEGY

This chapter outlines the basic framework and strategy for psychotherapy with the borderline patient. The details of the psychotherapy are elaborated in subsequent chapters. For relatively stable borderline patients, the psychotherapeutic process begins with a series of consultations, where the therapist takes a reasonably thorough history and discusses the arrangements and guidelines for the treatment. For patients entering treatment in crises or in regressions, the history-taking needs to be abbreviated, and the arrangements and guidelines are introduced piecemeal. In these instances, much of the introductory process is delayed, until some of the presenting issues have been addressed, and the patient is in a calmer state.

The therapist assumes a neutral stance and does whatever he can to promote a stable therapeutic environment. As the typical borderline patient has a major problem in forming and maintaining a therapeutic alliance, much of the early therapeutic work focuses on issues regarding the alliance. Whenever there is any disruption, the therapist needs to intervene actively to help strengthen the alliance. Insight-oriented techniques are used whenever possible. If these are insufficient, more supportive techniques are utilized. Whenever possible, the movement should be back to the insight-oriented techniques.

Ideally the transference is allowed to unfold and develop with little intervention. This ideal is rarely accomplished in the early phases, where both negative transferences and disruptions to the therapeutic alliance are the norm. Meaningful interventions regarding core difficulties can only occur when there is a workable therapeutic alliance; thus, they should only be initiated when the alliance is reasonable. By interventions regarding core difficulties, I refer to interventions other than those needed to deal with the negative transference and disrupted alliance. These latter interventions, of course, also refer to core problems of the patient. Typically there is an oscillation between focus on the therapeutic alliance and interventions involving other core difficulties. Unending sequences occur as follows. Disruption of the therapeutic alliance leads to focus on the disruption, followed by the strengthening of the alliance. This leads to an intervention regarding a core difficulty, which causes another disruption in the therapeutic alliance, with the above sequence repeating itself. To minimize disruptions, interventions are delivered with an empathic attitude, a neutral stance, in an affirmative way, with preparatory comments, and with input from the patient. With some borderline patients, there are such overwhelming problems in the area of the therapeutic alliance that it takes years of very difficult work to establish even a tenuous alliance. With these patients the major focus of the entire therapy can be on alliance issues. More frequently the alliance becomes gradually but increasingly stable, and the therapeutic focus can shift more and more to interventions regarding other core difficulties.

Interventions regarding core difficulties are classified in this book under several categories. These include anxiety and defense, primitive defenses, severe acting out, introjects, and reality testing. Although anxiety and defense are listed as a separate category, there is a preference for utilizing this conceptual framework when making any intervention. This way of thinking is particularly well known and utilized with neurotic patients. An upsurge in aggressive or sexual feeling is opposed by the superego. The ego responds by anxiety and then defense against the anxiety. The resulting symptom is a compromise formation by the ego in response to the aggressive or sexual feeling, the superego, and external reality. In using this conceptual framework the borderline individual differs from the neurotic in a number of ways. The anxiety is often more intense and difficult to tolerate. In addition to anxiety, more uncomfortable affect states, such as rage, embarrassment, shame, humiliation, and emptiness, are often experienced and defended against. The repertoire of defenses includes more primitive mechanisms and more acting out. Superego prohibitions can be harsher and more demanding, and there can sometimes be accompanying distortions in reality testing. With these differences, symptoms are formed in an analogous way to the neurotic individual. Correspondingly, interventions analogous to defense interpretations in neurotic patients can be effectively utilized. Sometimes these interventions need to be bolstered by titration of the frustration, utilization of the observing ego, and other more supportive methods.

One does not need to classify interventions in accordance with this book; neither does one need to employ a model emphasizing anxiety and defense. Other classifications and other theoretical models can certainly be substituted. The emphasis here is that the interventions regarding the core difficulties, via whatever classification and theoretical underpinnings, can only be effectively utilized when there is a reasonable therapeutic alliance. With the strengthening of the alliance, these interventions can be made in a variety of situations throughout the course of the psychotherapy. Interventions regarding the core difficulties, in addition to interventions addressing the disruption of the alliance, when repetitively made, provide for the possibility of change via insight. Change by insight and change by identification and internalization are the two mechanisms by which the borderline patient can improve his life.

In respect to interventions regarding core difficulties, as with interventions regarding disruptions in the therapeutic alliance, insight-oriented techniques are attempted first. Whenever these are insufficient, they are supplemented or supplanted by more supportive techniques. Wherever reasonable, movement is toward the insight-oriented techniques. It is the preponderance of the insight-oriented versus the supportive interventions that determines the overall coloring of the therapy. Some borderline patients do well with a primarily insight-oriented approach; others need many supportive mechanisms. There is wide variation here.

Although rapid mobilization of the transference is typical of the borderline patient in the early phase of psychotherapy, this proclivity sometimes changes after the establishment of a reasonable therapeutic alliance. One group of patients continues to use the transference as the main modality through which conflicts unfold and are resolved. For this group, modified analytically oriented psychotherapy is the treatment utilized. Although there is often an emphasis on insight-oriented techniques in this group, supportive interventions are often also needed. A second group of borderline patients, after much initial difficulty, maintains a relatively stable therapeutic alliance and then uses that alliance as a vehicle to explore core difficulties outside of the transference. Focus here is on the core difficulties as they play out in the workplace and with spouses, friends, and acquaintances. For this group, dynamically oriented psychotherapy is utilized, once the therapeutic alliance has stabilized. Here either insight-oriented techniques and/or supportive techniques can be used. With both modified analytically oriented psychotherapy and dynamically oriented psychotherapy, genetic material can be utilized in the latter parts of the therapy. The utilization of genetic material is another area of much variation within the borderline population.

15

LARGER ISSUES

STABILITY OF THE THERAPEUTIC ENVIRONMENT

Therapy needs to be carried out in a stable, consistent, and caring way in a safe, nonthreatening, and nonintrusive environment. The expectations of treatment should be clearly spelled out, discussed, and almost always followed. These details include times of the sessions, missed appointments, payments, expectations regarding interactions between therapist and patient outside the sessions, and guidelines for the patient. Stability of the therapeutic environment implies that the therapist is competent, consistent, conscientious, concerned, empathic, and reasonable. A stable, well-adjusted, and well-analyzed therapist is essential when working with a borderline patient.

The concepts of good-enough mothering and holding environment (Winnicott 1965) are relevant here. Adler (1985, 1993) particularly emphasizes these ingredients, although they are implicit to virtually all psychotherapeutic approaches. It is the stability of the therapeutic environment that is most instrumental in the gradual formation of a workable therapeutic alliance. The expectations of treatment noted above will be elaborated in Chapter 16, on "Arrangements."

NEUTRALITY AND FLEXIBILITY OF THE THERAPIST

When working with borderline patients, the therapist needs to maintain a combination of neutrality and flexibility. This is not a contradiction; the therapist can be both neutral and flexible.

Technical neutrality classically refers to the therapist's position of equidistance from id, ego, superego, and external reality. In dealing with borderline patients I view the concept of neutrality in a somewhat different way. A neutral therapist is one who stays clear of judgment and criticism. He aims to use the therapy session to listen to and understand the patient, and to make interventions based on this listening and understanding. This aim is emphasized and maintained throughout the treatment. Interventions always focus on the patient, his problems, and his life. Before intervening, the therapist thinks about how his intervention will influence the patient in the processes of internalization, ego building, and insight. Although the therapist will sometimes react emotionally to the patient, he uses his reactions to understand the patient as much as possible. Overidentification and excessive intrusion of the therapist's life into the therapy session are avoided. The neutrality of the therapist should be maintained as much as possible. The "as much as possible" needs to be emphasized, because with borderline patients, it is next to impossible to maintain this posture all of the time. Neutrality, as described here, does not connote lack of warmth, lack of empathy, or lack of flexibility.

Flexibility of the therapist is as essential as neutrality. The therapist has to be flexible with both approach and with interventions. He has to be ready for the unpredictable, ready for new challenges, and able to be intuitive. Although he needs to operate within a definite theoretical framework, he has to be able to make changes and adaptations within that framework. Depending on the unfolding of the therapy, he might need to change from an insight-oriented approach to a more supportive approach, or vice versa. With some patients, he will have to oscillate in his approach over long periods of time; with others, he might have to switch approaches permanently. Always he needs to be pragmatic and adaptive.

COUNTERTRANSFERENCE

Countertransference with borderline patients is emphasized by basically all therapists. Meissner (1993) considers it, along with the therapeutic alliance and the transference, as one of three legs of the therapeutic tripod in dealing with these patients. Borderline patients are known for their ability to elicit emotional reactions in the therapist, sometimes obvious but just as often subtle. It is not unusual for these patients to sense areas of weakness in the therapist and subtly attack the therapist in those areas. Thus, in working with borderline individuals, the therapist is especially vulnerable to countertransference acting out. Probably more therapies are ruined by countertransference reactions than by poor technique. With this mind, the therapist needs to be constantly vigilant to countertransference. With each and every thought about the transference and with each and every intervention, countertransference possibilities need to be consciously addressed.

In dealing with borderline individuals, it is best to speak of countertransference in the broad sense. This includes all emotional feelings by the therapist to the patient, both conscious and unconscious, rather than the therapist's unconscious reactions to the patient's transference. Gabbard and Wilkinson (1994) have categorized typical countertransference reactions to borderline patients. These include guilt feelings, rescue fantasies, transgressions of professional boundaries, rage and hatred, helplessness, worthlessness, anxiety, and terror. Some of these feelings are inevitable when working with borderline patients by all therapists; others occur more selectively with certain therapists working with certain borderline individuals.

All therapists are, at times, vulnerable to countertransference acting out when working with borderline patients. Because of this, even the most experienced therapists need to be willing to partake in consultations with colleagues. Well-timed consultations can be invaluable, sometimes "saving" the therapy. With less-experienced therapists, ongoing supervision is clearly useful. Obviously, one's own psychoanalysis helps with understanding and dealing with countertransference. The basic idea, of course, is to decrease countertransference acting out and to use one's countertransference feelings to help understand the patient.

ACTIVITY OF THE THERAPIST

It is often helpful for the therapist to take a more active approach, both talking more and using more facial expression, when dealing with borderline patients. This is particularly useful with patients lacking in both trust and self-esteem, with negative self-concepts. These patients respond to relative silences or to ambiguous comments by feeling criticized, slighted, or rejected. They respond this way either during the therapy hour or as delayed reactions after the hour. They often fantasize that the therapist thinks they are stupid, doesn't like them, prefers others, or doesn't want to see them anymore. Sometimes the fantasies are more ominous and paranoid. These fantasies can lead to very uncomfortable feeling states with acting out.

To help create a comfortable therapeutic environment, out of which a reasonable therapeutic alliance can develop, the therapist is best off initially with an interactive approach, with many clarifications, and as little ambiguity as possible. Later in the therapy, as the therapeutic alliance becomes consolidated, a gradual decrease in activity is often warranted.

A second group of patients who benefit from increased activity by the therapist are those suffering from feelings such as emptiness, nothingness, and apathy, related to childhoods lacking in excitement, vitality, and stimulation. A more silent therapist can revive and enhance those uncomfortable feelings, helping to create a therapeutic environment that resembles that of the early childhood. A more interactive approach can lead to a more comfortable milieu for the patient, again enhancing the chances of eventually achieving a reasonable therapeutic alliance. In both of the above situations, an interactive approach does not necessarily translate into the use of more supportive techniques. It is the quantity of interventions, not the type, that is of importance.

In contrast to the above patients, another group of borderline individuals, often with marked narcissistic traits, view interventions as unwanted intrusions. Very sensitive to being dependent, controlled, or violated, these patients act negatively and angrily to most interventions. In the early stage of therapy, these patients do better with a more silent approach, sometimes with minimal therapeutic activity. Later in the therapy, when the patient becomes comfortable and a reasonable therapeutic alliance has been formed, the therapist can become more active. The principle in all cases is not to do what the patient wants, but to promote a therapeutic alliance that will best facilitate the psychotherapy.

MECHANISMS OF CHANGE IN PSYCHOTHERAPY

There are two main mechanisms of change in psychotherapy: change via insight and change via the relationship. The first mechanism emphasizes interventions, particularly insight-oriented ones. The second emphasizes identification and internalization. Regarding the latter, change does not occur by any specific role played by the therapist; it takes place silently as the therapy unfolds in its natural way. Insight plays a larger role in psychotherapy with "healthier" patients; the relationship assumes greater importance with more "troubled" individuals. Yet, both of these mechanisms play important roles in all types of therapy. Regarding borderline patients, change by insight and change via the relationship can be considered a complementary pair.

16

ARRANGEMENTS

Arrangements regarding psychotherapy need to be discussed and established at as early a time as possible. These include scheduling of times, payments, missed appointments, expectations regarding interactions between therapist and patient outside the sessions, and guidelines for the patient.

SCHEDULING

Scheduling times convenient for both patient and therapist is, of course, ideal. From the therapist's perspective, the sessions need to start on time and end on time. From the patient's perspective, hopefully they will start on time, but whether they do or do not, they need to end on time. The ability and responsibility of managing time are integral to a structured and stable life. Adhering to the time agreements conforms with the reality of life in general. Thus, except in clear emergencies, there should be no deviations regarding extending the sessions.

LATENESS

Regarding lateness, minor characterological deviations need not be focused on early. With time, the patient will usually bring up the lateness himself, elaborating on such items as his desire to do one more thing, his tendency not to waste any time, his need to overschedule, and so forth. More significant lateness, however, can be a major resistance, requiring prompt attention and intervention. Discussion of lateness should initially be from the standpoint of anxieties that occur in the therapy that lead to avoidance of the sessions.

FIVE-MINUTE WARNING

Some borderline patients have difficulty leaving the session. The end of the session often feels like an abandonment or a rejection. The patient might say: "Don't you like being with me?" or "I know you can't wait to get rid of me so you can see your next patient." Various attempts to extend the hour, such as bringing up significant material near the end or waiting until the end to write the check, are well known. One method of dealing with this difficulty in select patients is the *five-minute warning.* Here the patient is simply told that there are five minutes left. This warning alerts him to speak of material he's excluded to that point. Additionally, it enables him to prepare himself for the separation and avoid the situation where he feels abruptly cut off. Discussion of the desirability of this parameter needs to precede its initiation. Often it can be abandoned later in the treatment.

INTERACTIONS OUTSIDE THE THERAPY HOURS

Regarding interactions between patient and therapist outside the therapy hours, the general rule is the less, the better. The therapist can make it clear that he welcomes and even expects calls at times of true emergency; otherwise he neither expects nor desires them. Emergencies necessitating calls need to be spelled out; many so-called emergencies can be easily handled without the therapist. The generalization here is that psychotherapy proceeds best when it is confined to the therapy sessions. If there is not enough time during the sessions, the frequency can be increased. On occasion, extra sessions can be scheduled in accordance with the patient's desires and "needs."

There are numerous exceptions. Some patients, for example, need very brief occasional contact to confirm the reality of the therapist. Others need various kinds of brief contact to avoid overwhelming anxiety. Under these circumstances, therapist and patient can arrange limited telephone conversations. Specific agreements regarding phone calls need not come up at the beginning of treatment, unless an obvious problem is anticipated. Discussion can wait until after the first or even second phone call. At that time the rationale for the limits can be stated and discussed. Firm limits set in a reasonable way can make the difference between virtually no phone calls or daily phone calls. To set these limits well, the therapist has to have good boundaries regarding the therapy hours himself, plus the belief and experience that therapy is best carried out when it is confined to well-defined sessions.

PAYMENTS

Payment arrangements need to be addressed early, including both fee and collection policy. Many therapists have some flexibility in their fees, with some ability to make adjustments in accordance with the patient's income. In these situations, frank discussions of the patient's finances and insurance coverage need to be part of the fee setting. It is important that both therapist and patient are comfortable with the fee. Therapists need to understand their own financial requirements in regard to fees, including under what circumstances they are willing to accept lower fees. Some patients will volunteer to pay more than they can reasonably afford. As this situation can rapidly undermine the treatment, it needs to be avoided. On the other hand, some patients try to pay as little as possible. A fee clearly too low can be indicative of a sense of entitlement and/or devaluation of the treatment. In cases of reduced fees, it is always good policy to allow for periodic re-evaluations.

A usual practice is to bill at the end of the month and collect shortly thereafter. Payment can be due the session after the bill, two weeks later, or a month later. Sometimes there is an agreement to wait until the patient has collected from his insurance. In this case, a reasonable policy is to be paid in a prescribed period of time (like one month) or whenever the insurance check arrives, whichever is first. This puts responsibility on the patient to send the bill in on time, call the insurance company when necessary, and so forth. Whatever the arrangements, they need to be clearly agreed upon. Deviations from the agreement then can be focused on in the treatment hours, as they occur.

MISSED APPOINTMENTS

Not long ago, the usual rule regarding missed appointments was for the therapist to charge unless he filled the time. A reasonable addition to this was that, given advance notice, the therapist was willing to reschedule, if possible. Although still reasonable in many cases, this rule appears to be going out of favor. Some therapists have a rather liberal policy of not charging if notice is given a certain number of hours in advance (like 24 or 72). Others do not charge if there is a good reason for the missed appointment. The latter is never a good idea. Illness, car problems, college examinations, or other important appointments, although reasonable on the surface, are often used as resistance. Evaluation of the reasons puts the therapist in the unwanted position of an authority figure, inviting the patient to rebel.

The variation of missing appointments from patient to patient is truly amazing. I have seen a number of patients who have never missed a session over a number of years of multiple sessions per week. Other patients miss regularly (several times a month), with reasons they feel are totally unavoidable and beyond their control. I have seen several patients who missed for very minor illnesses, acting as if this was totally reasonable and the norm. In these cases, this was related to concepts of themselves that were both quite fragile and also somewhat entitled. In the course of therapy, these images were able to be addressed and eventually modified. Regarding patients who never miss, occasional absences late in the therapy can be a positive sign, reflecting the relaxation of overactive super-egos.

The therapist can show some flexibility in establishing agreements regarding missed sessions. I favor telling the patient that my usual policy is to charge for missed sessions unless I fill the time, with the exception that I am willing to reschedule hours, if possible, when given advance notice. I state that I understand that whereas many patients understand such a policy, others have difficulty with it. Thus, if the patient has any misgivings about the policy, I am willing to discuss them. I do believe that my usual policy as stated above is beyond the experience of many patients. Some patients see the policy as overly rigid, greedy, one-sided, and unfair. With patients who are not able to understand the policy from the therapist's perspective, the policy is not a good one. In these cases, modifications are necessary. With some patients, where I sense that there will be clear antipathy toward the usual policy, I do not bring it up. If and when a problem arises, I approach it in a flexible manner.

The following vignette regarding Ms. C is the most extreme in my experience regarding the policy of paying for missed sessions. Therapy with Ms. C seemed off to an uneventful start, that is, until the fifth week or so. Earlier on I had told Ms. C that my usual policy was to charge for missed sessions, unless I could fill the time. I had said that I would be willing to discuss this if she had any misgivings about it, with the clear implication that there was flexibility for change there. When Ms. C offered no objections, we moved on. Then around the fifth week, Ms. C said she had been thinking about my fee policy, in fact had become increasingly obsessed about it. Her conclusion was that it was totally unacceptable. After considerable discussion, I said that although I had originally felt that the policy was reasonable, I could understand her objections, and because of those, the policy would not apply to her. This, however, did not eliminate the issue. The fee policy became the main topic, session after session. Despite our detailed discussions, Ms. C held the opinion that although the fee policy would not apply to her, it was nevertheless clear evidence that I was insensitive, unconcerned, inclined to treat her unfairly, and only interested in money. She thought it would be difficult to work with such a self-centered, unempathic, and money-oriented individual. As other evidence of my lack of concern and insensitivity entered into the hours, such as my letting her in a minute late on one occasion, my taking a week's vacation, and my occasionally moving about in a restless way, Ms. C concluded that it would be absolutely useless to continue treatment with me. After exploration of this, I referred her to a colleague.

Regarding another patient, I had to use some quick thinking regarding the fee policy. In this case, after a lengthy evaluation and after a thorough discussion of the guidelines regarding psychotherapy, including the fee policy, the patient said that he was ready to begin treatment. He entered the next session saying that although he was ready to begin, he refused to pay for missed sessions when he gave me reasonable notice.

Thinking as fast as I could, I suggested a modification of my usual fee policy: when the patient gave me advanced cancellation notice, the responsibility would fall on him to determine whether the cancellation was reasonable, and whether he should pay for the session. This agreement would be subject to review and revision by either of us. In this highly conscientious and motivated patient, this modification never became a practical problem. Actually, it enabled the patient's conflicts regarding the fee policy to enter into the treatment hours repetitively.

GUIDELINES FOR THE PATIENT

It is useful for the patient to be given a set of guidelines regarding psychotherapy near the initiation of treatment. The guidelines are similar to the basic rule of analysis, but with modifications applicable to psychotherapy. Similar to the basic rule of analysis, they establish a frame for the therapy, one that can be returned to whenever there is a deviation. Like Gray (1994), I do not present the guidelines as instructions or rules, finding that too authoritarian and rigid. It is puzzling to me that although standard for psychoanalysis, few therapists spell out such guidelines for psychotherapy. Kernberg (1989) is one clear exception.

A standard presentation that is useful for most borderline patients is as follows:

> *Therapist:* The sessions are yours, to talk about anything you want. It will be up to you to choose the topics. Often there will be topics that are on your mind that you very much want to talk about. At other times this will be less clear. At times when you do not have topics of pressing importance, it is helpful to talk freely about anything that comes to mind. In fact, whenever you have extraneous thoughts or fantasies, it is useful to talk about them. Please try to be as open as possible. There are

> certain thoughts that some people find difficult to talk about and are tempted to omit. I want to urge you to do your best not to omit those types of thoughts. These include thoughts that cause uncomfortable feelings, such as anxiety, anger, embarrassment, or shame, thoughts that you view as silly or irrelevant, thoughts that you are fearful that I will disapprove of, and any thoughts, positive or negative, that refer to the therapy or to me personally.

As noted, once the guidelines are established, they become useful reference points, to return to whenever there is a deviation. Thus, if a patient, after a month or so, says nothing about the therapy, the therapist might make the following comment.

> *Therapist:* I want to bring up one item. When we started therapy, I mentioned that one of the things that would be useful to hear about was any thoughts that you had, either positive or negative, about the therapy or about me. You haven't said anything about that, and I was wondering about your thoughts on that topic.

As a discussion about this unfolds, the therapist might inquire about what inhibited the patient from bringing up that topic himself.

CONTRACTS

Regarding arrangements at the outset of psychotherapy, I find those just enumerated—scheduling of times, payments, missed appointments, expectations regarding interactions between patient and therapist outside the sessions, and guidelines for the patient—more than adequate. They both provide a useful frame for the treatment, and are not too cumbersome or detailed for the patient. Longer and more specific contractual agreements, if needed, are often best initiated later in the therapy. Many borderline patients enter treatment with some urgency, in some state of crisis or regression. They are preoccupied with their problems and want to address them as soon as possible. They have little tolerance for negotiating contracts until there is some focus on their presenting complaints. For these patients, even the arrangements enumerated above can be burdensome, seeming like a distraction. For a patient in this category, I introduce the guidelines piecemeal, after some of the presenting issues have been addressed, and when the patient is in a calmer state. The patient is then able to approach the arrangements both with more interest and more cooperation.

Issues elaborated in longer contracts, as I have already noted, are better addressed later. Not only is the patient better able to deal with them, but the therapist has had more time to understand the patient's dynamics. Increased understanding of the dynamics obviously makes for better contractual agreements. Obvious exceptions occur when the problems are introduced immediately and are of the nature that demand rapid attention. Items of this nature include overt suicidal tendencies and any acting out that might rapidly undermine the therapy. Chronic, less dangerous forms of acting out can be addressed later, as they enter the therapy hour spontaneously. The technique of pointing out specific negative experiences in past therapies and the possibility of their recurrence in the current therapy is an excellent early intervention. However, it need not be part of a contract.

Contracts often provide a false sense of security to the therapist. They have little validity without a reasonable therapeutic alliance, and as noted, this takes time. It does little good to set up agreements, if the patient is to ignore them as soon as he is in a different frame of mind. Unfortunately, this is the case with many borderline patients whose moods shift rapidly. At the time of the contract, the patient might fully believe that he will, without fail, call the therapist or go to the emergency room if he feels actively suicidal. Then when he is actually overcome with strong suicidal feelings, the contract loses its meaning.

When using a contract, the therapist should never set up agreements that he is apt to negate. I have heard examples of contractual agreements to terminate treatment after several suicide attempts. Then after the attempts, he therapist feels differently and continues the work. Basically, I would never set up a contract where the consequence is termination. Likewise, the therapist should not set up agreements where the patient is required to forego behavior that is related to his core psychopathology. The patient is unable to keep such an agreement. The principle here is simple. All individuals have tendencies and propensities to certain symptoms, certain forms of acting out, and certain behavioral patterns. No matter what they are, they recur under stress. It is only through a thorough understanding of the stresses in psychotherapy or by an elimination of them in the real world that the symptoms and behavior patterns can end.

17

THE THERAPEUTIC ALLIANCE AND THE TRANSFERENCE

The therapeutic alliance is the collaborative relationship between patient and therapist, established to facilitate the work of psychotherapy. It demands that the patient maintain an observing ego that continually focuses on the therapeutic process. This observing ego is in alliance with the therapist against the patient's conflicts and resistances. Although it can include unconscious components, the therapeutic alliance operates mainly on a conscious level. In contrast, the transference is an unconscious process, in which the patient, in a regressed state, displaces or "transfers" onto the therapist feelings and thoughts that were originally directed toward the important people of early childhood. The transference includes not only these feelings and thoughts, but also defenses against them. It is based on both the actual and fantasized past, as experienced by the patient.

THE THERAPEUTIC ALLIANCE

Typically, the borderline patient has a major problem in forming and maintaining a therapeutic alliance. This poses a major difficulty in the therapeutic work, one that needs to be focused on repetitively and continuously. Some feel that it is only near the end of the therapy that the alliance becomes reasonable and workable. Exceptions to these generalizations include patients at the high end of the borderline spectrum, who typically exhibit fewer alliance problems. In marked contrast to the usual borderline individual is the neurotic patient, where a strong therapeutic alliance is basically a given.

With the borderline individual, the alliance is typically fragile and tenuous initially, becoming increasingly stronger gradually and incrementally with much regression and progression. Factors discussed in Chapter 15, regarding the stability of the therapeutic environment, are the basic ingredients that help strengthen the alliance. Thus, the alliance is strengthened as the patient experiences the therapist over time as being stable, competent, consistent, conscientious, and concerned. Under the influence of these factors, the therapeutic alliance automatically develops without active intervention.

Whenever there is any disruption in the alliance, the therapist needs to intervene actively. He needs to point out to the patient that there is a problem with the therapeutic alliance and to invite him to explore this difficulty. Disruptions in the alliance need to be addressed, repetitively, throughout the therapy, whenever they occur. The therapist might make a comment similar to the following.

> *Therapist:* There seems to be a problem with the two of us working together most effectively. Do you agree? I wonder if there is something I am saying or doing that is contributing? Could we talk about that?

In the early stages of therapy, in eliciting the cooperation of the patient, it is helpful to place the responsibility more on the therapist. Later, as the alliance becomes progressively strengthened, more responsibility can be placed on the patient.

Continuing with the above example, the patient might respond:

Patient: Actually now that you mention it, I am bothered by the way you keep turning the air conditioner off and on. When I say it, it sounds silly. I know you're trying to get the temperature right. Yet it bothers me. Also, I hate it when you move around in the chair. You don't do it so much, yet it's still annoying.

Here the patient focuses on some surface complaints about the therapist. A response early in treatment should stay on the same level, as follows.

Therapist: I'm sorry that what I do is bothersome. As you've already guessed, there isn't a thermostat here, and you're right about my moving about. I'll try to refrain from that as much as possible, and I will also try to stop playing with the air conditioner. I'm glad you were able to bring this up. Let me know if this again becomes annoying. For that matter, please tell me anything that bothers you here.

Only later in the treatment are factors within the patient that contribute to the annoyance focused on and explored. Thus, an example taken from a patient in therapy for a number of years is as follows.

Patient: The problem with you is that you don't listen to me and empathize with me. You're more interested in some little detail. And I find that so infuriating! Haven't you ever read Kohut? All I want you to do is to listen and to be empathic. Is that asking too much? All I get from you are these obsessional details.

In response, the therapist first notes that he doesn't want to sound defensive, but that he thought he was listening. He also was trying to be empathic. He does understand that it can be annoying when he focuses on a detail, rather than on how the patient feels. He then goes on to explain why he focused on the particular detail. The patient is satisfied with his explanation, and patient and therapist are able to explore the detail at length. After this, the therapist returns to the patient's sensitivity about his "not listening and being empathic." The patient is now able to explore her early upbringing where her parents didn't listen empathically and were more interested in the details of their own lives than in being in tune with their daughter.

In this example, there was a temporary disruption in the therapeutic alliance based on what the patient perceived as a lack of empathy. Here the therapist was able to address the disruption, regain a reasonable therapeutic alliance, and then to help the patient to focus on her role in the disruption.

Regarding the vignette, repetitive occurrences of the above type of interaction, with recurrent clarification and focus on the patient's sensitivities as a child now being played out in the transference, were met with both a gradual lessening of these sensitivities in the patient and a continued strengthening of the alliance.

A reasonable therapeutic alliance is a precondition for the therapist's interventions to be effective. Typical of many borderline patients is a gradual improvement in the alliance, with much waxing and waning. Thus, there is often an oscillation between focus on the therapeutic alliance and focus on interventions involving other core difficulties. As noted in Chapter 14, unending sequences often occur as follows. Focus on the therapeutic alliance after a disruption is followed by a strengthening of the alliance, leading to a therapeutic intervention involving a core difficulty. The latter intervention causes another disruption in the alliance, and the above sequence repeats itself. As the therapy progresses and the alliance becomes increasingly stable, there is more focus on the other core difficulties and less focus on the alliance.

Patients who have difficulty in establishing and maintaining the therapeutic alliance typically have had childhoods where there were inconsistent, unstable, and unreliable figures with whom to identify. Adler is helpful here when he talks of the problem of the borderline patient in attaining stable holding introjects. The attainment of stable holding introjects parallels the ability to maintain a stable therapeutic alliance.

THE TRANSFERENCE

Consistent with the borderline diagnosis is a rapid involvement with the therapist and the transference. Although there are exceptions, such as with withdrawn, isolated, and schizoid borderline individuals, this rapid transference involvement is typical. In accordance with this involvement, the initial stages of treatment usually take the form of a modified analytically oriented psychotherapy. One group of borderline patients continues to focus on the transference throughout the therapy, making the analytically oriented approach the treatment of choice. A second group of borderline patients, after a reasonably stable therapeutic alliance has been established, switches away from the emphasis on the transference. For this group, the analytically oriented modality changes to a more dynamically oriented approach.

The rapid mobilization of the transference distinguishes the typical borderline patient from the typical neurotic. Neurotic patients become involved with the transference at a slower and more gradual pace, at times with some difficulty. Psychoanalysis provides a forum for these patients that enhances the development of a regressive transference. The borderline patient, in contrast, easily regresses and easily focuses on the transference without psychoanalysis.

There are several generalizations regarding the transference. Whenever possible, the transference should be allowed to unfold and develop without intervention. However, whenever the transference becomes negative and/or interferes with the therapeutic alliance, rapid intervention is necessary. Unexplored negative transferences often lead to unwanted acting out, directly threatening and undermining the therapy. Thus, even subtle indications of negative transference need to be addressed. Positive transferences that are either overtly idealized or overtly eroticized are generally handled in a similar manner to negative transferences. In these cases, the speed of the intervention is less important, as destructive acting out does not occur as rapidly. No intervention is needed regarding the mildly positive portion of the transference that contributes to the therapeutic alliance. Mild to moderate idealizations can likewise usually be left alone, at least initially.

Interventions here can often be confined to some combination of clarification, confrontation, and interpretation. It is only when these types of insight-oriented techniques are ineffective that more supportive interventions (to be spelled out in the next chapter) are needed. Examples of interventions regarding the transference are provided in the forthcoming chapters. In Chapter 21, on "Primitive Defenses," there are several examples dealing with negative transferences. Two of these examples involve severe devaluations, where reasonable interventions proved to be ineffective. In Chapter 19, on "Anxiety and Defense," the vignette of Ms. G provides an example where repetitive interventions were needed to keep the patient in therapy, when she globally attributed her intense anxiety and psychosomatic symptoms to the transference. In Chapter 21, an example of a typical intervention with a very primitive idealization is provided. Additionally, a vignette is presented where a mild to moderate primitive idealization was maintained throughout the course of an eight-year therapy. In Chapter 20, on interventions regarding severe acting out, the example of the young accountant demonstrates an unanalyzed mildly idealized transference that contributed greatly to the therapeutic alliance.

Regarding eroticized transferences, when they occur early in the treatment and are mild, they sometimes contribute to a positive attitude toward psychotherapy. Often these transference feelings are unexpressed and innocuous, becoming diminished with time. More overt expressions of eroticized transferences need to be addressed. Subtle hints or overt expressions of sexual acting out between patient and therapist are somewhat common between those male patients who typically sexualize relationships and women therapists. A comment by the therapist such as: "It seems easier for you to express your sexual feelings to me than to address the problems that brought you here," or "You seem more comfortable flirting with me than in talking about your problems in forming long-term relationships," is often all that is needed to overcome this type of resistance. With more persistent demands for sexual acting out, a more definitive technique, often including limit-setting, is required. If a patient thinks that sex is a real possibility, the reality and rationale for its prohibition need to be discussed.

Several examples of rather striking eroticizations follow. The first involves a borderline patient whom I was seeing in intensive psychotherapy for over a year. One day at the beginning of a session, this patient calmly announced that she was really "horny" and that she wanted to have sex with me. She elaborated both her reasons and the sexual acts she had in mind. I first commented on how this request seemed like a resistance to working on her problems, and then elaborated one reason after another why sex would not make sense psychotherapeutically. To each reason I gave, she had a rebuttal. After exhausting every imaginable idea that I could think of, she stated, "But it'll only take a few minutes!" Needless to say, there was no acting out.

Another patient, overtly psychotic and being seen in a hospital setting, rapidly undressed after entering my office. Thinking rapidly, I stated that I would leave the office briefly and when I returned, I expected her to be fully clothed. When I returned in five minutes, she had complied with the request.

The final vignette also took place in a hospital setting. This time I was acting as interim therapist to a chronically psychotic but reasonably intact patient. In our first session, she entered my office and immediately announced that she had decided that it would be therapeutic for her to have sex with me. After I went through my usual reasons why this could not happen, she said that we still should do it. Her reasoning was that on her way to my office, she had passed Dr. H, who had raised his little finger in such a way that clearly signaled to her that she should have sex with me.

The above three vignettes are extreme and unusual. Rarely are patients so persistent in their eroticized demands. Usually they respond well to conventional interventions.

18

INTERVENTIONS

TYPES OF INTERVENTIONS

Insight-Oriented Interventions

The interventions of clarification, confrontation, and interpretation are the ones most usually associated with insight-oriented work. Confining oneself to these interventions enables the therapist to maintain technical neutrality.

Clarification (Bibring 1954) means to see things in a clearer way. It refers to matters that are conscious or subconscious, but not unconscious. Clarification helps the patient to become clearer about feelings, attitudes, thoughts, behavior patterns, and perceptions. The therapist often uses clarification to help the patient bring together contradictory attitudes, behavior, and ideas.

Confrontation is a subgroup of clarification (Meissner 1980). Clarification usually appears more neutral on the part of the therapist, whereas confrontation involves a more intrusive stance. Confrontations are sometimes designed to create conflict where there previously had been none.

Interpretation (Bibring 1954) strictly deals with unconscious material. It can refer to both defenses and that which is defended against. It often provides an explanation or a hypothesis about conscious behavior. Interpretations are often preceded by numerous clarifications.

Examples:

1. Clarification (of splitting)

The patient described Pam as shallow, insensitive, and generally reprehensible.

> *Therapist:* Wait a minute. Is that the same Pam that you described last week as one of the most wonderful people in the world?
>
> *Patient:* Yes, that's her. What of it?
>
> *Therapist:* I can't help but notice the rapid change in your thinking about her. Last week she was your best friend. Today she's despicable.

2. Clarification (of self image)

> *Patient:* You know, doc, I'm just a little weakling. I don't exercise, I don't diet, I become short of breath when I walk a block. I don't know if I can survive. What if someone tried to rob me? I couldn't defend myself.
>
> *Therapist:* You present yourself as little, helpless, and weak. What do you think about that self-image?

3. Clarification (of inferior-superior introjective pair)

> *Therapist:* When you calmly state, as if it's a fact, that your wife is not curious about things and that she won't consider any change whatsoever, you convey the impression that you view her as an inferior person. At that moment, you seem to view yourself as superior.

4. Confrontation (of denial)

Patient: (after his seventh overdose) Doc, I feel great! This will never happen again. I can absolutely assure you of that!

Therapist: I don't want to be blunt, but you are using extreme denial. Just because you're feeling good at this moment, you insist that it will never happen again.

5. Interpretation

Therapist: Could it be that your tendency to seek out such exciting and dangerous activities, in addition to your propensity to choose only the most exotic and sensual women, are both ways of avoiding and defending against those horrible feelings of emptiness and nothingness?

With borderline patients, clarifications and confrontation predominate over interpretations. Typically, few interpretations are made in the early stages of the therapy. As the therapy progresses, and the therapeutic alliance is strengthened, interpretations become more common. I cannot stress enough that this is relative. Opportunities present themselves for some interpretive work throughout the course of therapy with most borderline patients. Likewise, with selective borderline individuals, there can be more emphasis on interpretation from early on.

Initially, interpretations are usually made in the here and now. Although genetic interpretations are not typically made in the early phases of treatment, they need not be avoided, especially with those occasional patients who present this kind of material. The rule of thumb is to follow the patient. If he brings up relevant genetic material, at any time, it is certainly allowable and often helpful to comment on it. Inexact interpretations (Glover 1931) are sometimes useful. Here deeper unconscious material is not directly interpreted; instead, derivatives of that material that are more acceptable to the patient are addressed. Examples include speaking to the patient's assertive qualities rather than his murderous rage, or to his masculine characteristics instead of his latent homosexuality.

Supportive Interventions

There are many other interventions used in the psychotherapy with borderline patients. These include suggestion, therapeutic manipulation, abreaction, advice, reassurance, education, limit-setting, reality testing, and giving encouragement and praise. Unlike clarification, confrontation, and interpretation, these interventions, if used with any frequency, are more typical of supportive work. When used extensively, they preclude neutrality.

This is a good time to review the concept of the borderline continuum or spectrum. As noted, borderline patients can be best thought of as a heterogeneous group, occurring on a spectrum of levels and degrees of pathological personality functioning. The higher end of the spectrum merges with narcissistic and neurotic patients, whereas the lower end merges with psychotic patients. All patients on the spectrum are characterized by some combination of ego strengths and ego weaknesses, as elaborated in Chapter 1. Yet, each patient is a unique individual, with his own combination of strengths and weaknesses, his own unique personality, and his own unique behavior patterns.

Strategy regarding Interventions

The closer the patient comes to the neurotic end of the spectrum, the more the therapist should focus on insight-oriented interventions. Even here, there often needs to be a supportive empathic environment that makes therapy different from that with a more typical neurotic patient. At times of regression, limit-setting, suggestion, and advice are needed, but in general, supportive types of interventions are minimized. Correspondingly, the closer the patient is to the psychotic end of the spectrum, the more the therapist needs to focus on supportive techniques. Suggestion, advice, education, limit-setting, and therapeutic manipulation play a larger role here. In general, I do not find much use in extensive praise, encouragement, or reassurance. Subtle varieties of reality testing, in the form of offering alternate possibilities or perspectives of the self, others, and/or the external world, can be quite useful. This technique will be discussed further in Chapter 23 on interventions regarding reality testing.

In initiating psychotherapy, I try to have as few preconceived ideas as possible, allowing the transference to unfold and selecting my interventions in accordance with this unfolding. The initial stance is one of exploration and clarification; deviations from this are in accordance with occurrences within the therapy hours.

If by clarifications alone the patient is reasonably comfortable, talkative, and motivated, no other interventions are needed. Whenever there is an obstacle to this positive position, attempts are made to resolve the obstacle. Insight-oriented techniques are tried first. If these are insufficient, more supportive techniques are utilized. Thus, if the patient is decently talkative with a mild idealization of the therapist, the therapist might confine himself to clarifications. If the patient refuses to leave the office after the session, the therapist might revert to suggestion and limit-setting. If the patient seems very perplexed with the therapy, the therapist might add a bit of education.

Despite clear definition, interventions can and do overlap with each other. Some patients frequently "hear" one intervention when the therapist intends a different one. In some ways, suggestion is the polar opposite to interpretation. Yet, interpretations are sometimes understood and responded to as suggestions. I recall one example where there were months of clarifications and interpretations regarding a patient's tendency to be attracted to troubled, needy, and exotic women, while avoiding more stable professional ones. In the therapy, this was related to the patient's oedipal fears and fears of success, with the recovering of early childhood memories regarding fears of attacks by the father. After months of interpretive work, the patient said:

> Patient: So what do I make of all this? What is the message that Dr. G is giving me? Ah, I've got it!! He wants me to stop going around with those women that I meet at the dances and to start dating Jewish doctors and lawyers.

THE FORM OF THE INTERPRETATION

The manner and style in which the intervention is delivered, in addition to the wording, is of obvious importance. An empathic attitude with a neutral stance is always desirable. A confrontational, aggressive, or defensive stance is to be avoided. Before making any intervention, one should try to be as free of feelings as possible. It is common to offer an interpretation when one has been provoked, in the guise of helping the patient understand. The unconscious motive of the interpretation is retaliation. Although interventions made in this manner might well be accurate, they usually lead to arguments and battles, greatly detracting from the therapeutic alliance. Alternatively, supportive interventions are often offered prematurely when one either feels guilt or openly sympathizes with the patient. A good rule of thumb is *not* to offer any intervention when one is feeling any strong affect. Simply wait and think!

In the following example, it has already been established that Jacob is Jewish. In the vignette, the therapist is also Jewish.

> *Patient:* (laughing) Jacob, the handyman, came over the house the other day. You really have to be careful when he gets

in the house. No matter what, he'll find something to fix. Wants to get me to pay him as much as possible.

(A little later) Irv told me that after the [Jewish] service, he got together with a group of friends and talked about how they could make more money. Making money seems to be their number-one priority.

Therapist (feeling attacked himself): You seem to be very picky today. First you come in and don't bother to close the door. Then you spend five minutes criticizing the book you see on my desk, going out of your way to discover the title. Then you make several hostile comments about Jews. What are you so angry about anyway?

A better comment than this very defensive confrontation might have been:

Therapist: A number of times in the past when you have expressed criticism of Jews, it turned out that you were angry at me. Do you think that could possibly be happening here now?

The first response, made with an edge, invites more criticism and a battle between patient and therapist. The second offers an opportunity for more collaborative exploration.

In the next example, the patient appears soaking wet.

Patient: (coughing and complaining) It was so difficult getting here. I left my umbrella at work, then had to walk two blocks to your office. And I'm just getting over a cold. I just feel so bad (sobbing a bit)! I wish I could have a cup of hot chocolate.

Therapist: I don't have any hot chocolate, but I can offer you a cup of coffee. And here, have a cough drop.

Although the therapist's response here doesn't seem so unreasonable, it does not offer the patient a chance to explore any transferential feelings related to her feeling victimized. Had the therapist not responded so reflexively, the theme of blaming the therapist for the inconvenience might well have come up. This would have allowed the exploration of the victim role in the transference. Depending on a number of factors, being supportive might not be contraindicated. What was contraindicated was the therapist acting so rapidly and so much in accordance with her own feeling. If done repetitively, important themes would not enter into the therapy.

Returning to the style and manner of the intervention, Meissner (1988), as noted in Chapter 12, focuses on Schaffer's (1986) concept of affirmative interpretations. Affirmative interpretations are made in such a way that they are experienced as empathic and respectful. They often demonstrate an appreciation for what the patient is experiencing, and are usually well received. The importance of this concept when dealing with borderline patients is self-evident.

Preparatory Comments

A related strategy that I use is what I call preparatory comments. Here the therapist, anticipating a negative reaction to his intervention, prepares the patient by comments before the intervention. There are a wide variety of negative responses the therapist might anticipate to his interventions. The patient might feel slighted or rejected, insulted or criticized. He might feel misunderstood, or become unreasonably angry or guilty.

In all cases, the anticipated negative reaction is based on responses to similar interventions in the past. The preparatory comments pave the way for the patient to be able to listen and respond to the intervention with a minimum of defensiveness. As the treatment progresses, these preparatory comments become less necessary. Often the patient will let the therapist know when they are no longer needed.

Examples:

1. *Therapist:* I want to say a few words before my question. The last time I commented on a financial matter, you felt that I was showing off, demonstrating to you that I knew more than you about money. I want to assure you that I do not have the intent. With that in mind, I was wondering about your reasoning when you refused to use an accountant for your taxes.
2. *Therapist:* I have a feeling that you might object to this comment because it focuses on the transference. You've told me time after time that it's ridiculous to emphasize the transference, that you didn't come here to explore your relationship with me. Nevertheless, it might be useful to pick up on your earlier allusion that your dating the internist might have something to do with me.
3. *Therapist:* I know you view yourself at times as unaccomplished and inadequate, and I know that you hate it when I think of this as your view of yourself rather than reality. Nevertheless, when you say that you can't possibly take that job, I was wondering if that might have more to do with your sense of being a "loser" rather than with the actual difficulties involved in the work.
4. *Therapist:* I want to say that I do not mean to be competitive with you. Actually, it's clear that you know more about internal medicine than I do. Yet, I was wondering if your thinking that Bob should be placed on blood pressure medicine had more to do with your dislike of and anxiety about dietary restrictions (for yourself) than on Bob's minimally increased blood pressure.

And last, late in the therapy:

5. *Therapist:* I just want to say a few words . . .
   Patient (interrupting): I know, I know. You want to be certain that I don't interpret your comment as insulting. I've heard that a hundred times. Just get on with your comment. I get the point already.

Input from Patients regarding Interventions

Borderline patients often distort the therapist's interventions, either with and especially without preparatory comments. Because of this, the patient's understanding of the therapist's intervention needs to be regularly examined and clarified. The patient frequently need to be asked his thoughts and feelings about an intervention, and then the therapist might comment on the patient's remarks. With some patients this process needs to take place on a regular basis. In asking for patient feedback, the therapist should start by being rather general. Depending on the patient's response, he then can become more specific.

Example 1: The therapist's intervention is followed by a period of silence.

Therapist: What do you think about the comment I just made?

Patient: It seems reasonable enough to me. (The patient then goes on to another topic.)

Therapist: I notice that you're going onto another topic. Yet, I would like to return to my comment for a minute. I was wondering what feelings you had about what I said.

Patient: Well, to tell the truth, I thought it was a correct observation. But haven't we been over that before? It's not like you're telling me anything new. So what's the point?

In the above example, the patient defended against his anger by avoiding any comment on the therapist's intervention. The therapist had to ask the patient to comment on his intervention twice before the patient finally responded with emotion.

Example 2:

Therapist: What do you think about the comment I just made?

Patient: I think you're full of shit. I never think that way. The idea that you think I'm that uncaring is very upsetting.

Therapist: I didn't mean that you were uncaring. It's already crystal-clear that you are a very caring individual. I only meant that for one minute you seemed to focus on your own thoughts and lost track of what your student was saying. (The therapist then goes on to elaborate on the specifics here.)

Patient: Oh, I see what you mean. I guess you're right. I thought you were being very critical, but now I see that you're not. I didn't want to get angry at you, so I changed the topic. But I guess I really was angry.

Example 3: This occurs after the therapist asks the patient to comment on his intervention, and the patient responds in a reasonable way.

Therapist: The last time I made a comment like that one, you had the idea that I was acting like a know-it-all, like your father.

Patient: That's true, and I felt that way again. But it was to a lesser degree. Actually, I think I'm at the point where I can catch myself doing that, then not feel that way.

The first example did not include any distortion. The patient merely suppressed and avoided her anger by changing the topic. The second example involved a clear distortion of the therapist's intervention, where the patient felt severely criticized. The third example involved an appropriate response to the therapist's intervention. Here the therapist followed up, because the patient had acted severely to similar interventions in the past.

There are some patients who initially respond reasonably to an intervention. Then, after the hour, they distort some aspect of it and become upset. Where this is a pattern, it is important, after the initial response, to point out the patient's tendency for delayed responses.

Therapist: Your response to my comment seems very reasonable. Yet I can't help but remember that the last time I made

> a similar comment, you told me that you couldn't sleep at all that night, and it was because of my comment. On that occasion you thought I was demeaning you, but you only had that idea after the session.

One of my patients often distorted what I said, to almost psychotic proportions, months after the intervention. Sometimes she would quote me quite incorrectly. She would say that she was almost certain that I had said what she claimed. All I could do was to say that my memory of my comment was different from hers, stating what my memory was. Then I invited her to explore our differences in memory, so that we could possibly arrive at some better understanding of the intervention. On one occasion I presented the hypothesis that maybe she had projected her thoughts onto me. This opened the door to a general discussion of her projective tendencies in relation to distortions of my interventions.

Another patient once surprised me by telling me that he had followed my suggestion and had attended a party over the weekend, and that it had gone quite well. When I mentioned that I hadn't recalled making that suggestion, he was as confused as I was. Much later we were able to figure out what had happened. This patient had a habit of asking me for confirmation of what he had just said. I often commented that his ideas sounded reasonable or that what he said certainly was one possibility, or something analogous. When I offered such a confirmation to the patient, he then attributed the comment to me rather than him. By this mechanism he would forego any responsibility and remain passive. With discussion the patient was both able to understand the mechanism of the distortion and some of the dynamics underlying it. In the above example, the patient had told me that he wanted to go to the party and was certain it would be useful to him. When asked, I had said that his ideas sounded reasonable. It wasn't until there were several other examples of this type of projective mechanism that I was able to understand what was happening and discuss it with the patient.

19

ANXIETY AND DEFENSE

Interventions with neurotic patients regarding defenses against anxiety are commonplace. Neurotic anxiety typically involves castration fears, fears of punishment, fears of loss of love (and rejection), and sometimes fears of loss of the object. This type of anxiety typically surfaces when one is pursuing a relationship with the opposite sex (or a homosexual relationship), when one is trying to advance himself competitively in the workplace, or when one is asserting himself in any situation. Psychoanalytically, this relates to the upsurge of a drive (sexual or aggressive feeling), opposition by the superego to the drive, the creation of anxiety in the ego, and a defense against the anxiety. One notes this sequence both inside and outside the therapy hours and makes interventions, often interpretive. One usually interprets the defense against the anxiety before what is defended against.

The borderline patient can experience similar kinds of anxiety. However, the anxiety is often more intense and more difficult to tolerate, and the superego prohibitions against it can be harsher and more demanding. Additionally, the repertoire of defenses includes more primitive mechanisms. Sometimes the reality basis for the anxiety is analogous to the neurotic patient; at other times, the reality basis can be quite distorted. Thus, some patients experience intense anxiety about fantasized relationships where there is no actual involvement. Others become acutely anxious in work situations about what seems to be trivial items. One patient acted out suicidally to a perceived rejection by a movie actress to whom he had never talked. Another became almost immobilized with fear when he learned that he would have to carry mail to the third floor, in addition to his usual delivery to the second. Despite the differences in intensity of anxiety, harshness of the superego, repertory of defenses, and the reality basis of the anxiety, interventions analogous to the defense interpretations in neurotic patients can and should be made.

A patient, a talented young man with a college degree and a number of strengths, nevertheless experienced several hospitalizations for suicidal ideation and attempts over the years. He was now in a halfway house, had a temporary job, and went out regularly with a girlfriend. Whenever confronted with any task involving progress, he would invoke an image of himself as helpless, pathetic, inadequate, and weak. Sometimes the self-image would be quasi-delusional, as when he would claim that he had literally lost all his strength. He could not lift a 10-pound bag of groceries; if someone would push him lightly, he'd fall down, and so forth. This "pathetic" self-image arose when the patient left the hospital for the halfway house, when he acquired his temporary job, and whenever he had occasion for any assertive behavior.

Now the patient was just offered a different job, in an area that he had not worked before, but in an area easily within his abilities.

Patient: (walking into the office slowly with a dejected air) You know, doc, I'm just a little weakling. I don't exercise, I don't diet, I become short of breath when I walk a block. I don't know if I can survive. What if someone tried to rob me? I couldn't even defend myself.

Therapist: Again, you present yourself as little, helpless, and weak. What do you think that's about?

Patient: (getting a bit annoyed) It's not a presentation, doc. That's the reality! You never believe me! But it's true. If someone tried to rob me, I'd just be defenseless. (The patient escalates as he insists on the validity of what he is saying.)

Therapist: You don't appear so little and weak when you argue with me and try to force me to agree with your image of yourself as pathetic.

Patient: (laughing) I hate that term "pathetic."

Therapist: So what do you think this image of yourself as little and helpless is all about?

Patient: (laughing) I know, doc. It's the new job. I just don't think I can do it.

After a lengthy exploration of the anxieties associated with the job, the therapist returns to the patient's self-image.

Therapist: So we see that, again, whenever there is a chance to move forward, you become overwhelmed with anxiety. Your response to that anxiety is to invoke what we call "the little self-image." It's easier to think of yourself as incapable than to move forward in the face of the anxiety you experience.

Although the patient was quite fragile, the therapist was able to make an intervention involving anxiety and defense that was similar to typical interventions with neurotic patients. It might be noted that the turning point in the intervention was the interpretation of the (unconscious) interpersonal interaction component of the projective identification, when the patient insisted that the therapist agree with his self image. In this vignette, the (unconscious) fears regarding moving ahead were unusually strong, leading to intense anxiety. The defense of invoking a "pathetic" self image was accompanied by a defense of withdrawal and some distortion of reality. The actual reality of the situation, confirmed later, was that the patient had no difficulties with the new job. I will return to this vignette in Chapter 23, when I discuss interventions regarding reality testing.

UNCOMFORTABLE AFFECT STATES

In addition to anxiety, there are other affect states that borderline patients find quite uncomfortable. These include rage, embarrassment, shame, humiliation, excitement, and grandiosity. These affect states occur most frequently in those borderline patients with narcissistic traits, who are especially vulnerable to perceived slights, rejections, rebuffs, and disappointments. More so than anxiety, these affects can be excruciatingly painful and difficult to tolerate. Thus, they are defended against rapidly. The patient often defends against these feelings by a variety of self-soothing and acting-out behaviors, including increased activities of many sorts, stimulating and dangerous acts, perverse sexuality, and alcohol and drug abuse.

In the psychotherapy sessions, these affects can be dealt with similarly to anxiety. Interventions involving anxiety (or uncomfortable affect state) and defense are often reasonable and useful. In the sessions, the dysphoric affects need to be experienced and tolerated as much as possible. This tolerance must be followed by careful exploration of what frustrates the patient and how he typically responds to the frustration. The sequence of frustration, followed by uncomfortable feeling state, followed by defensive acting out, needs to be repetitively addressed. Sometimes this type of exploration can be augmented by an additional focus on the maladaptive consequences of the defensive behavior. When this is done, care must be taken to maintain a neutral, nonjudgmental, and noncritical stance.

Dr. L, a middle-aged, moderately successful physician, was incredibly sensitive to being treated unfairly, with a tendency toward rapid rage on these occasions and ensuing acting out. All this happened almost at a stimulus–response level. For example, a truck driver cut off Dr. L and within seconds he challenged the driver to a fight. On another occasion, a colleague treated Dr. L discourteously on the phone, to which Dr. L uttered a few choice words and hung up. Work in the therapy sessions focused on attempts to slow down these stimulus-response-type reactions. As one example after another came up, Dr. L gradually was able to experience and tolerate painful feeling states that corresponded to his being treated so unfairly. As he began to replace his usual acting with thinking, he was able to link these uncomfortable shameful feelings to previously unconscious self representations of being inadequate and passive, maybe even homosexual. Genetic exploration traced this to repetitive experiences of being embarrassed and even humiliated by his father. With years of focusing on the sequence of frustration, uncomfortable feeling state, painful self representation, and defensive acting out, Dr. L was able to alter his usual impulsive behavior. Psychotherapy with Dr. L took place somewhat in accordance with the model of defensive change via insight. In this example, understanding occurred without direct reliving of the experiences in the transference.

Mr. V was a young lawyer to whom stimulation became a way of life. Although functioning in a superior manner professionally, nights and weekends were filled with excitement and stimulation. After work, Mr. V would head to the bars and to the dance halls, where he sought exotic and attractive women. These women, typically unstable and needy, formed clinging and dependent relationships with Mr. V rather rapidly. Weekends were spent at other forms of recreation: mountain climbing, biking, boating, and caving. Vacations were used to go on cross-country bike trips or abroad to the most exotic countries. Mr. V viewed these activities without anxiety and as commonplace.

Occasional breaks from these nonstop activities led to feelings akin to emptiness or nothingness. Mr. V came to appreciate that ordinary activities did not help rid him of these uncomfortable feelings, nor did the usual professional women with whom he regularly associated. He "needed" stimulation and activity well beyond the ordinary. The therapist was able to help Mr. V to understand that the stimulating activities and exotic women were ways of dealing with these very uncomfortable feelings. Mr. V described a childhood devoid of fun and amusement, where everything was totally serious. With this atmosphere, related to tragedies that both of his parents had suffered, Mr. V early on sought out both soothing and excitement. As Mr. V was able to identify his feelings of emptiness and nothingness, to relate these feelings to his childhood environment, and to understand his tendency toward stimulating and exciting activities and people as a defense against those feelings, he was gradually able to turn to events and people at least somewhat more ordinary. By the end of therapy, Mr. V had married an "ordinary" professional woman and had replaced the stimulating activities by more exciting aspects of his profession.

The model of therapy with Mr. V was in accordance with change via interpretation of dysphoric affect and defense. Although Mr. V was not typically borderline, his dysphoric affect of emptiness, his defenses against it, and the psychotherapeutic intervention utilized are typical of borderline individuals. The role of the therapy itself as stimulation and excitement entered the hours near the termination of Mr. V's treatment.

A final example is afforded by Ms. G, a woman similar to many individuals written about by Giovacchini (1993a). This patient experienced difficulty with continuity, problems experiencing and identifying feelings, difficulty correlating present and past, and problems in understanding casual links. Ms. G was prone to periods of overwhelming anxiety and to psychosomatic symptoms, of which she was unable to attribute any cause. At times she experienced a blank feeling or a void. Somewhat like Mr. V, she engaged in a variety of stimulating and, in her case, often dangerous activities. These included parachuting, rock climbing, and boat trips down dangerous rapids. On a number of occasions, there were accidents with severe injuries.

At the beginning of psychotherapy, Ms. G had no idea that there might be a linkage between her internal feelings and these dangerous activities. As might be imagined, the initial transference theme was an inability to experience any feelings toward the therapist. While there was a devaluation of the therapy in words, with an expressed lack of understanding of how the treatment worked, there was evidence that the therapy played an increasingly vital role in Ms. G's life. Having difficulty with cause and effect, Ms. G began to attribute any feelings and occurrences in her life to the effects of the therapy. This was done in a global way and was certainly not in accordance with reality. Thus, if Ms. G had several good weeks, she would attribute that to the therapy. Likewise, psychosomatic symptoms and intense anxiety were attributed to the treatment. At these latter times, Ms. G experienced intense urges to terminate.

There was a necessary initial focus on alliance problems, as they continuously threatened the treatment. Whenever there was a reasonable modicum of therapeutic alliance, there was focus on experiencing and identifying feelings, and then correlating these feelings with precipitants. This took place mainly within the transference, and was a very slow and tedious process. As the alliance was gradually strengthened, both by factors emphasized in Chapter 15 regarding the stability of the therapeutic environment, and by focus on disruptions in the alliance, there was more sustained work on the central issues. Ms. G gradually was able to link specific perceived slights, criticisms, and lack of interest by the therapist with dysphoric feelings. She experienced feelings of embarrassment, shame, and humiliation in response to these slights and criticisms, but defended against these almost instantaneously. She likewise experienced a void, or a blank feeling, to a perceived lack of interest by the therapist. As the work progressed, Ms. G was able to become more specific and less global in cause and effect regarding her feelings.

It was only after several years of the above type of work that Ms. G began to learn to correlate her painful feeling states to

> defensive activities. Linkages between uncomfortable feelings and rapid defense were only able to be initiated after linkages to precipitants (or frustrations) and feelings were established. Of course, linkages of frustrations to feelings could only be accomplished after Ms. G was able to experience and identify her feelings. Thus, initial focus was on experiencing and identifying feelings. This was followed by focus on linking these feelings with precipitants. Finally, linkages of the feelings to defensive acting out took place. As noted, all of this work could only be accomplished at times of a viable therapeutic alliance, taking place after much focus on alliance problems. By the end of a prematurely terminated treatment, Ms. G had some awareness of the correlation of her feelings (anxiety, embarrassment, shame, humiliation, rage, emptiness) to both her psychosomatic symptoms and to her stimulating activities.

This vignette again demonstrates the need for viable therapeutic alliance if therapeutic interventions are to be reasonably utilized. Only when the alliance is sufficiently stable can insight-oriented interventions be used in a meaningful way. In this example, interpretive types of interventions involving the model of anxiety (or uncomfortable feeling) and defense were able to be accomplished after much difficult preparatory work. With Ms. G, the primary work took place within the transference.

TOLERATION OF THE FRUSTRATION

Interventions regarding anxiety (or uncomfortable feeling) and defense, especially within the transference, can sometimes be associated with affect states that become quite painful and unbearable. In those instances, to avoid unreasonable disruptions, the therapist must keep watch on the amount of frustration in the therapy sessions. Hence "titration" of the frustration in the therapy hours is sometimes necessary, in addition to exploration. On occasion, despite all efforts, acting out is of such magnitude that limit-setting and structuring of the patient's life outside the therapy hours becomes necessary. This includes the use of day centers or even hospitalization. Temporary hospitalization at times of regression allows the therapy to continue with greatly reduced risks of disruptive behavior.

UTILIZING THE OBSERVING EGO

In therapeutic work involving anxiety (or uncomfortable feeling) and defense, an observing ego is necessary. By this observing ego, the patient is able to stand back from the conflict, observe, and try to understand what is taking place. Sometimes a patient is able to comprehend the dynamics, yet at times of stress, loses the ability to maintain the observing ego. Then, the symptom or disruptive behavior occurs despite the understanding. In these instances, the therapeutic focus needs to be on maintaining the observing ego.

> Mr. H, a high-powered achievement-oriented professional, continually set up exalted, idealistic, and often very unrealistic aspirations and goals. He felt obligated to fulfill these goals at all times without exception. When he failed to meet his expectations, he criticized himself in the harshest and most relentless way. He would verbally berate himself, at times for hours. These verbal "beatings" took the form of accusing himself of being undeserving, inadequate, a piece of trash. He shouldn't have been born; he deserved to die! "Beatings" took place for a variety of events, ranging from not achieving more at work, not being a better son or friend, or seemingly insignificant items, like not cleaning his room or failing to exercise. At times, Mr. H "beat" himself for having physical difficulties, such as headaches or the flu.
>
> In the course of therapy, Mr. H was able to arrive at a fair amount of insight. He understood the idealism and the grandiosity behind his unreasonable goals. He understood the ex-

treme harshness and viciousness of his superego attacks. He understood the gratification involved in these attacks, and how they could be sexualized at times. He understood that the "beatings" stopped him from moving forward in work and with relationships. He understood the triggers and precipitants to the symptoms. He had a decent understanding of the genetic correlates to the problem, including specific early memories involving his parents and brothers. Although ameliorated somewhat in frequency and intensity, the "beatings" continued.

At this point, therapeutic focus changed to an examination of how, despite his understanding, the symptoms recurred. There was a direct focus on the observing ego. What stopped Mr. H from using his observing ego to take a look at what was happening, gain perspective, and take action to stop his symptoms? Exploration revealed that the failure to involve the observing ego was itself a passive defense against being assertive. The above type of exploration allowed Mr. H eventually to gain more control over his symptoms.

With Mr. H, the therapy, including the focus on the observing ego, remained at an exploratory level. Sometimes the work of invoking the use of the observing ego utilizes more suggestion. This more supportive approach is turned to if a more exploratory approach, like that with Mr. H, has been unsuccessful.

This chapter has focused specifically on interventions regarding anxiety (or uncomfortable affect) and defense. Actually, this particular conceptual model can be used with regard to any intervention. Thus, interventions regarding primitive defenses, severe acting out, introjects, and reality testing can all be framed around this conceptual modality. Although many other ways of thinking are useful and reasonable, there is a preference in this book to frame interventions along the model of anxiety and defense.

20

SEVERE ACTING OUT

Regarding the psychotherapy situation, acting out technically means to act as opposed to talk. In a more general sense, it is used to refer to overtly action-oriented behavior rather than symptoms or behavior traits. In a more specific sense, it refers to action-oriented behavior that is particularly self-defeating and self-destructive, such as suicide attempts, acts of physical aggression, and dangerous activities. It is acting out in this latter specific way that is the focus of this chapter. As a defense, acting out can be conceptualized dynamically like other defenses: as a compromise formation by the ego in response to the drives, the superego, and external reality. Thus, interventions regarding acting out can be framed in accordance with the model of anxiety (or uncomfortable affect) and defense.

Regarding interventions, insight-oriented techniques are attempted first. Although these are often successful with severe acting out, at other times they fail and need to be supplemented or supplanted by more supportive methods. As noted in Chapter 19, acting out is sometimes of such magnitude that limit-setting and structuring of the patient's life outside the therapy hours become necessary. This includes the use of day centers or even hospitalization. Temporary hospitalization at times of regression allows the therapy to continue with greatly reduced risks of disruptive behavior. This chapter focuses on severe acting out that does not respond to insight-oriented interventions alone.

VIGNETTE #1

A young accountant was involved in several incidents of unfortunate acting out, in efforts to ward off acute anxiety and fears of catastrophe. He had left his previous job abruptly, after his anxiety rose to an intolerable level. He had then wandered around the country for several months, gradually calming down. Recently he had taken a job similar to the first one. Sensing his anxiety level again beginning to rise, he entered psychotherapy.

Regarding the previous job, on the surface things had gone well. The accountant was well liked, did good work, always acted agreeably and accommodatingly, and had been promoted rather rapidly. Yet he had become increasingly anxious and uncomfortable. He was particularly bothered by a lack of an overtly positive attitude by his boss and by a perceived lack of appreciation by his colleagues. He wanted his boss to give him regular feedback, make sure he had the best working conditions, offer advice, give praise when appropriate, and in general to act in a fatherly manner. He wanted his colleagues to appreciate his skills overtly, to offer encouragement, and to reach out to him socially.

It wasn't that his boss and colleagues weren't positive to him; in fact they were. However, both disappointed him in accordance with his idealistic and unrealistic expectations. Additionally, the young accountant began to question some of the goals and values of the company. He felt the company should be more efficient, more productive, and more organized. He felt it would be in the company's best interest to be more sensitive to the needs of the employees, and he had no understanding why that wasn't emphasized. He realized that the company's values weren't so bad; yet they were far from his ideals.

As his expectations remained unfulfilled and he became increasingly disappointed and discontent with the various perceived deficiencies of his workplace, the accountant began to experience a lack of energy, enthusiasm, and well being. He began to brood, and then became overtly angry. Work felt more and more negative to him, and he began to dislike being there. As his anger increased, he became anxious that he might have a major confrontation, with fantasies of getting fired or of fist fights. When the anger and anxiety reached an intolerable level, he abruptly quit.

Socially the accountant had been dating a young woman for several years. The relationship was reasonable, mutual, and intimate. When the idea of marriage came up, the patient began to feel panicky. He was worried about all sorts of issues, from the type of wedding ceremony to the raising of the children. He began to feel coerced and forced to marry against his will, with fantasies of being made passive and weak. Ultimately he feared that marriage would be a catastrophe, limiting his freedom and individuality. As his anxiety increased, he abruptly ended the relationship.

The young accountant began therapy in a very tenuous and ambivalent way, missing a number of sessions, typically being late, and continually talking about quitting. After this shaky start, he settled down and gradually formed a mildly idealized transference, out of which a reasonable therapeutic alliance developed. Needless to say, the greater part of the early phase of therapy focused on the strengthening of the alliance. With time, the patient began to feel that the therapist understood him and was appreciative, supportive, and empathic of his needs. Within that setting, he began to focus on difficulties and conflicts with his new job and with his new girlfriend. The conflicts that were instrumental in ending his previous work situation and relationship reoccurred. This time the patient was able to explore them, in a supportive environment, so that he did not act out. By a process of continual clarification of his conflicts and with intermittent definitive suggestion (not to abandon under frustration either the job or the girlfriend), the patient was able to move ahead in both areas. With time the suggestion (not to act under frustration) was no longer needed.

Regarding the work situation, the young accountant learned that his ideals and expectations were far too idealistic and far too unrealistic. Although reasonable on the surface, what he wanted and expected just did not happen in the real world. Although the ideal boss might call his employees in for frequent evaluations, give them encouragement and praise, and make sure their working conditions were optimal, bosses rarely acted like that. Although ideal friends might treat their co-workers with sensitivity, appreciation, and respect, the usual milieu in the patient's workplace was more likely to include sarcastic comments and competition. Although an ideal company might be most interested in accommodating its employees, the patient's company, typical of others, was more interested in its profits. As the patient began to realize that his expectations were related to his underlying desire and "need" to have a totally concerned, supportive, appreciated, and empathic father, he was able to lower these expectations and become more accepting at work. As noted, the therapist was perceived as a concerned, supportive, appreciative, and empathic father, although he never acted any differently than a reasonably skilled, dedicated, and concerned therapist.

Regarding his relationship with his girlfriend, as the possibility of permanency came up, the accountant again became increasingly anxious. He felt that marriage would close off opportunities, and he fantasized numerous catastrophes.

Again he entertained fantasies of being coerced and made passive by his girlfriend. Actually the girlfriend was quite giving and flexible, most frequently capitulating to the patient's wishes. Conflicts about feeling forced, coerced, and made passive (in relationship to the girlfriend) were brought into the therapy and examined. The patient's marked vulnerability in this area was noted, together with the reality of his dominance *vis-à-vis* his girlfriend.

Alternative possibilities to his fantasized catastrophes of the marriage were presented. The fact that the patient had run from several other relationships was noted and explored. Reasons for ending the current relationship were noted to be related to the patient's conflicts rather than the girlfriend's characteristics. At one point, it was noted that this particular girlfriend might have characteristics that actually complemented the patient's conflicts. Thus, with repetitive clarification, offering alternative perspectives (as will be discussed in Chapter 23 concerning "Reality Testing"), and with an overt suggestion (not to run), the patient was able to pursue the relationship, ultimately deciding on marriage. In the 6 months preceding the marriage, the therapist refrained from additional suggestions. Regarding the discussion of the relationship, the patient felt supported by the therapist, who was again seen as a mildly idealized father figure, interested in the patient's needs, showing respect for his conflicts, and appreciating his points of view.

Although it has not been emphasized in this vignette, work with the young accountant included a genetic component focusing on the father. Viewed as unsupportive, unempathic, and lacking in many ways, the father had the habit of exposing his son to the most anxiety-provoking situations. The son would feel coerced to participate in activities against his will, resulting in states of acute anxiety. Still the father was admired and idealized, and the patient was clearly disappointed and devastated by his early death. Genetic material regarding the father was related in the therapy hours to the patient's ideals and expectations with peers and supervisors, to his tendency to feel coerced, forced, and made passive, and to his proclivity for episodes of acute anxiety and fears of catastrophe.

The psychotherapy with the young accountant began by focusing on a very tenuous therapeutic alliance. After many interventions aimed at strengthening the alliance, related to numerous disruptions, a mildly idealized transference evolved, along with a good therapeutic alliance. The idealized transference was helpful in the maintenance of the therapeutic alliance and was left largely uninterpreted. Interventions were mainly insight-oriented, taking the form of understanding via the model involving anxiety and defense. To block destructive acting out, however, both suggestions and reality clarification in the form of offering alternate perspectives were utilized. The treatment, starting in the framework of a modified analytically oriented approach, evolved into dynamically oriented psychotherapy.

VIGNETTE #2

Dr. T, after a number of productive years of psychotherapy, casually announced that several months previously, he had visited a homosexual porno theater and, while in the bathroom, had engaged in fellatio. As there has been no evidence of either homosexual tendencies or acting out in this middle-aged, married man, this episode came as a total surprise.

The therapist first focused on Dr. T's failure to inform him of the event, noting that Dr. T had never talked about attending homosexual porno flicks or of homosexual fantasies. He wondered if something inhibited Dr. T from discussing these topics. Dr. T stated that he had been embarrassed about the act, and perhaps that was why he avoided talking about it. He had discussed the possibility of homosexual tendencies with his previous therapist, who had been emphatic that Dr. T was not homosexual. Dr. T agreed with this, as he had never experienced homosexual fantasies.

The therapist focused on strengthening an already decent therapeutic alliance, so that Dr. T would, without fail, bring all thoughts about porno flicks and homosexuality into the sessions. To be "certain" that this material was included, the therapist added the parameter of directly inquiring about these issues every few weeks. With this focus, relevant material gradually flowed into the therapy sessions. After much exploration, it became clear that going to the porno flick was motivated by feelings of shame, embarrassment, disgust, and rage for failing to complete an important project at work. In response to those feelings, Dr. T evoked an image of himself as inadequate, useless, and despicable, someone who needed to be punished. On an unconscious level, Dr. T felt that the best way to accomplish this punishment was by a homosexual act. It was as if Dr. T were saying to himself: "You are despicable for dropping the project. I'm going to punish you in a way that is clearly shameful. You'll learn your lesson and never fail at work again."

Dr. T was not aware of any of these dynamics before detailed exploration in the psychotherapy. In the treatment, Dr. T was able to re-experience the previous repressed painful affect states, then to link them to both the precipitants and the acting-out behavior. Genetic material regarding a very sadistic father who demanded perfection in school, then shamed and sometimes brutalized Dr. T when he was not compliant, added to his understanding. One of the father's favorite methods of shaming was to dress his son as a girl and call him a "sissy." Left out of the understanding of the dynamics was any reference to possible homosexual impulses, an area considered too frightening and too "unconscious" at the present time. Thus, the understanding, although accurate, was not necessarily complete, akin to an inexact interpretation as discussed in Chapter 18.

In this vignette, the therapist went beyond suggestion to help Dr. T experience and talk about his fantasies. The therapist took over the role of Dr. T's superego, insisting that he talk about relevant material. "Coerced" in this way, Dr. T responded. Through clarification and inexact interpretation, Dr. T was able to acquire dynamic understanding of his acting out. With this understanding, the acting out abated.

VIGNETTE #3

A teenage patient with intermittent suicidal ideation had been in psychotherapy for a number of years. Initially she concealed her suicidal ideation. On several occasions, she came close to acting, but fortunately her plans were discovered by the therapist in time for preventative hospitalizations. As might be evident at this point, the establishment of a therapeutic alliance was quite difficult, with several brief terminations in the early years. Later when the alliance became stronger, the patient was able to share her symptom of intermittent auditory hallucinations with the therapist.

With the sharing of the voices, patient and therapist were able to establish a sequence that the voices followed that allowed for early hospitalization at times of clear suicidal threat, before there was legitimate risk of acting. The voices started as sounds, then progressed to inaudible words, and then to words that the patient could hear but that had no understandable meaning. The words then took on meaning, but the meaning was vague. Then there were vague suicide ideas, followed by clear suicide ideas, followed by commands. In the command stage, the patient at first did not listen to them, but then was worried that she might. Of interest was the fact that the patient never thought the voices were of other people; she always maintained reality testing in that she viewed the voices as her own.

As the patient was able to reveal the above sequence, it became rather obvious at what point hospitalization was needed. With the establishment of the sequence, patient and therapist felt comfortable working on the dynamics of the voices without fear of acting out. As the dynamics were elucidated in the therapy sessions, the sequence would stop, usually with the voices decreasing in the same order in which they had originally occurred. Precipitants to the voices were learned about first and then the vulnerabilities underlying the precipitants. As understanding increased, the voices decreased, so that by the termination of therapy, they had virtually ended.

In this vignette, the severe acting out could only be contained after a suitable therapeutic alliance was established. At this point, therapist and patient were able to work collaboratively to use the sequence of voices as signals to impending acting out. As the voices came closer to signaling action, either dynamic understanding was successful enough to send the voices in the opposite direction or hospitalization was mutually agreed upon. Before the emergence of a reasonable therapeutic alliance, only hospitalization could prevent action. In this vignette, the possibility of hospitalization plus the establishment of a reasonable therapeutic alliance combined to make dynamically oriented therapy workable.

VIGNETTE #4

In the case of another teenager, several suicide attempts occurred without any warning, necessitating rapid hospitalization. It is always comforting to realize that one can hospitalize a patient to avoid acting out. In this case, there was no such comfort; the hospitalization followed the acting out. Here there were no signals, just action, almost on a stimulus–response level. Suicide attempts involved precipitants that took place outside of the therapy hours, related to various rejections and abandonments by boyfriends. The issues involved were not mentioned in the sessions, leaving the therapist helpless to intervene until after action had already occurred. Exploration of how such significant material was left out of the hours was pursued. Being very early in the treatment, this had little effect, as the patient at this point experienced minimal attachment and alliance with the therapist.

Later in the therapy, after the therapist had become a more important person to the patient, the precipitants switched to occurrences within the hours, usually to perceived slights, failures in empathy, and to abandonments (vacations). Although this switch put additional stress on the therapist, it also allowed for an examination of the relationship of the precipitants to the acting out. One day when the patient did not show for her session, the therapist, already forewarned that she was upset about an upcoming vacation, phoned her at her home during the usual therapy hour. The patient answered in a groggy state, having just swallowed a number of pills. She readily agreed to immediate hospitalization. This suicide attempt was despite previous detailed discussion about the therapist's vacation.

Exploration of this attempt revealed rage at the therapist for leaving the patient "at the worst possible time." The patient fantasized that the therapist would rescue her and then cancel his vacation to take care of her. The therapist saw the patient several times in the hospital and then arranged for a substitute therapist while he was away. The substitute became a permanent alternate therapist for the patient. Whenever the therapist was absent, the patient had "mandatory" sessions with this alternate. Although the intervention led to some splitting, it was greatly helpful in stemming the severe acting out at times of perceived abandonments.

As the conflicts centered more and more on the therapist, the therapy became both more stormy and more productive. Direct focus on the perceived slights, rejections, and abandonments by the therapist, together with the addition of the alternate therapist at the most stressful times, allowed for the exploration of the painful affects associated with these slights. For the first time, the patient was able to experience these painful affects long enough to talk about them without acting and to link them to their precipitants. By the end of a somewhat abbreviated therapy, the life-threatening and dangerous acting out had basically subsided.

In this vignette, the interventions of intermittent hospitalizations plus the addition of a "mandatory" substitute therapist were necessary to prevent extreme acting out. With these interventions, therapist and patient were able to explore some of the patient's core conflicts as they entered into the transference in an insight-oriented manner. In this example, definitive work could only be accomplished after the therapist became an important figure to the patient. After this occurred, she easily transferred her conflicts onto him, making transferential work both easy and profitable.

21

PRIMITIVE DEFENSES

The borderline patient, especially at times of stress, uses a number of primitive defenses. These include splitting, devaluation, primitive idealization, projection, projective identification, denial, omnipotence (Kernberg 1967, 1975), and various forms of acting out. At times of great stress, regression can lead to the use of psychotic defenses. When any of these defenses contribute to a negative transference or create a resistance to therapeutic work, rapid exploration is necessary. This is especially true regarding splitting, devaluation, denial, projection, and acting out. Idealization, omnipotence, and grandiosity also need attention, but focus here can often wait until later, when there is a better therapeutic alliance. Mild forms of idealization can sometimes be used to help strengthen the alliance.

The use of primitive defenses is almost always maladaptive and destructive to the patient's life. Thus, one of the aims of psychotherapy is to point out these defenses and their negative consequences, so that the patient can become aware of them and eventually decrease their usage. Primitive defenses should be demonstrated, both inside and outside the transference, whenever reasonable. Regarding outside the transference, this can be done leisurely with regard to the status of the therapeutic alliance. Interventions regarding primitive defenses can often be framed along the conceptual model of anxiety (or uncomfortable affect) and defense.

SPLITTING

The patient described Pam as callous, insensitive, and generally reprehensible. She said that Pam was basically a horrible person and that people like her don't deserve to be alive.

> *Therapist:* Wait a minute. That isn't the same Pam you described last week as one of the most wonderful people in the world, the Pam you found so helpful when you were studying for your French final?
>
> *Patient:* Yes, that's her. What of it!
>
> *Therapist:* I can't help but notice the rapid change in your thinking about her. Last week she was your best friend. Today she's a despicable character.

This is an example of splitting outside of the transference. After demonstrating the splitting mechanism, the therapist can begin to help the patient identify the events that precipitate the flips in the splitting.

Continuing with the present example:

> *Patient:* I guess you're right. I hadn't really thought of it that way. It is kind of striking.
>
> *Therapist:* I wonder how you came to see Pam so negatively?
>
> *Patient:* (thinking) Well, you know, I think I have an idea. I started really to detect Pam when she called at the last minute to cancel last weekend. She had a decent reason, but it didn't matter. I had looked forward to going out so much; then my

weekend was ruined. How could she do that to me? I felt she didn't care about me at all.

Therapist: You were looking so forward to the weekend. Then when Pam canceled, it was so frustrating that you switched from viewing her as one of your best friends to hating her.

Patient: Now that you put it that way, you're right. I really did change my feelings.

After a number of examples of splitting, the therapist can generalize the patient's tendency to use the splitting defense, sometimes with its consequences.

(Later in the therapy with the above patient):

Therapist: You've now presented a number of examples where you flip-flop drastically in your feelings about people. The same person who was recently a great friend becomes an enemy. And always the flips to the negative are precipitated by feelings that you've been rejected, criticized, or slighted. Sometimes you act negatively to those who have frustrated you and are later sorry. I remember you were quite upset when Pam wouldn't have anything to do with you for a month.

An example of splitting within the transference led to the following simple therapeutic intervention.

Therapist: I'm glad you feel so positively toward me now. Yet bear in mind, just two weeks ago you were so frustrated with me that you were ready to quit! Maybe we can look more closely at how your feelings toward me change so rapidly.

PRIMITIVE IDEALIZATION AND DEVALUATION

Primitive idealization can sometimes rapidly change to devaluation under the influence of frustration. At other times, the idealization, especially when on the mild side, can last almost endlessly. When a very primitive idealization enters the transference, it is helpful to point it out, with the warning that idealizations that come on rapidly can end just as rapidly, sometimes with devastating consequences. It is useful to explore the history of previous idealizations at that time.

> *Therapist:* It's nice that you think so positively of me. But I wonder about your idea that I'm one of the leading therapists in the world, and that as long as you're in my presence, everything will be fine. Sometimes when someone has such great expectations of another person, it doesn't take much to disappoint them. Then when they become disappointed, there can be severe reactions.
>
> *Patient:* But I'm sure you won't disappoint me. I am just convinced that I've found the perfect therapist.
>
> *Therapist:* I wonder if you'd had that feeling before?
>
> *Patient:* Well, actually yes!

As idealizations and devaluations are the positive and negative parts of splitting, interventions regarding splitting are often made when one of these defenses occurs.

A patient was extremely negative to his therapist. He stated that she really wasn't a good therapist. She wasn't qualified, she wasn't well read, and she didn't seem too smart. He wondered why he stayed with her. At times she seemed cruel.

> *Therapist:* You seem to think so poorly of me today. It's so different from last month, when you thought so highly of me. Any ideas about the dramatic change?
>
> *Patient:* Well, actually, I was really pissed when you didn't offer me an umbrella in that storm. I didn't ask, but it still seemed cruel.

An example of an intervention in an advanced stage of therapy regarding the chronic use of devaluation follows. The intervention goes beyond devaluation, pointing out the patient's corresponding grandiose stance.

> *Therapist:* When you calmly state, as if it's a fact, that your wife is not curious about things and that she won't consider any change whatsoever, you convey the impression that you view her as an inferior person. At that moment, you view yourself as superior and your wife as inferior. I can't help but think that this attitude toward your wife is related to what you see as her chronic passive aggressive stance to you.
>
> *Patient:* Could it be that it's the other way around, that I'm responding to years of hostility from her?
>
> *Therapist:* I guess that's possible. Yet we've seen that arrogant haughty attitude by you with other people. It's come up with me, as we've discussed.

I saw one patient who maintained a mild to moderate primitive idealization throughout the course of eight years of therapy. She maintained this at all costs and at all times. On occasion, she distorted reality so she could maintain the positive image of me. I recall one time when her teenage son told her that I had called the house and instructed him to tell her that I wanted her to be especially nice to him regarding school problems. For some reason, the patient never questioned the validity of the call, nor was she angry at me for either violating our agreement not to call her at home or for making such a ridiculous phone call. Instead she assumed that I had her best interests at heart and that I called because I thought it would be best for her if she treated her son better.

I offer the following vignette involving the use of a fairly mild idealization mainly for entertainment value.

The patient, a neurosurgeon, had been seeing me for a number of years. It goes without saying that his income at least doubled mine. In the middle of a session, he said: "Why does G do this? Why does G see me? I know, it's for the money. I think G sees me just for the money. Let me see." He then calculated my yearly income by multiplying my full fee by 50 hours per week, then by 50 weeks per year, obviously coming up with a highly inflated number. He paused and then said, "No, G can't possibly do it for the money!"

One of the most difficult types of referrals is when the patient has experienced years of marked primitive idealization with his previous therapist. I have been the recipient of two referrals of this sort, and neither worked out. One patient devalued me from the moment she walked through the door. The basic complaint was that she found me stupid in comparison to her past therapist. I had heard a number of complaints about myself, sometimes for not being empathic or giving enough, but never for being stupid. In a way that made this complaint easier to deal with, because I wasn't tempted to believe its merits and could concentrate on the devaluation. I told the patient that I had been criticized for not being empathic or warm enough, but never for being stupid. She responded that she found me very warm and that, in fact, she liked me. It just was that I was intellectually dull and if not stupid, certainly not very bright. This stance was used to devalue virtually anything I said. Of course, I pointed out how difficult it must be to see me after years of work with a therapist that she found so brilliant and intuitive. I also wondered if it might not be difficult for her to see anyone after her former therapist. I pointed out, in a nice way, the possibility of some idealization of her past therapist and some devaluation of me. Despite numerous interventions, which I thought were on target, the devaluation continued. Finally, I recommended a transfer to another therapist, and the patient agreed. Parenthetically, this is the only time I have initiated a transfer in circumstances of this sort. It's obviously much better to help the patient work out the problems in the transference.

In the second example, the devaluation was more indirect and more subtle. The patient didn't find the location of the office optimal, he didn't like the carpet, but most of all he didn't like the chair. He felt his chair was positioned lower than mine, connoting that I was superior and he was inferior. Then there was something bothersome about me that he couldn't put his finger on. I noted the latter as something worthwhile to explore. Additionally, I focused on the superior–inferior feelings. Again I noted how difficult it must be seeing a new therapist, after years of such positive work with another. The patient said he was tempted to leave but didn't want to, because I came so highly recommended. Also, he was unclear why he was so uncomfortable with me. He wanted to explore things more fully, as did I, but he left precipitously.

DENIAL

Primitive forms of denial often demand confrontation. This approach is not always helpful, because the patient often continues with his denial. Yet more subtle approaches are usually useless.

One example is provided by a young man who, awakening from a coma in the intensive care unit of a hospital after his seventh overdose, said: "Doc, I feel great! This will never happen again. I can absolutely assure you of that!"

> *Therapist:* I'm really happy that you're feeling so well. Yet I have to question your statement that you are absolutely certain that it will never happen again. I don't want to be too blunt, but you are using extreme denial. Just because you're feeling good at this moment, you insist that it will never happen again. What happens the next time you feel bad? Unfortunately, I wish I were wrong, but I can almost assure you that it will happen again unless you do everything you can to prevent it.

Confrontations similar to the above are often needed with patients who deny their alcohol or drug problems, and avoid therapy at all costs.

PROJECTIVE IDENTIFICATION

According to the Kleinians, psychotherapy works by an unending series of projective identifications. The patient projects onto the therapist, interacts with the therapist in some way, and then reintrojects or reinternalizes the projected part after it has been processed and modified by the therapist. As the reinternalized projection is an altered or modified version of the original projection, the patient changes accordingly. Thus, change takes place in psychotherapy by this process of projective identification without overt therapeutic intervention. The term *container* (Bion 1967) has been used to refer to the therapist who can tolerate and contain the projected feelings, including distress, chaos, hostility, neediness, and for that matter, love.

In addition to the silent change that takes place via projective identification, the therapist can make active interventions (usually interpretive), demonstrating this mechanism. Regarding projective identification, it is the interpersonal interaction component that is most conducive to initial intervention. One example of this has been presented in Chapter 19, on interventions regarding anxiety and defense, regarding the talented young man with numerous hospitalizations for suicidal ideation. This young man perceived and presented himself as weak and helpless.

The therapist directly pointed out the patient's projective identification when he said:

> *Therapist:* You don't appear so little and weak when you argue with me and try to force me to agree with your image of yourself as pathetic.

In case 2 in Chapter 5 on "Projective Identification," the patient presented herself as inadequate and then did everything she could to force that view onto the therapist. Here the therapist might have responded as follows.

Therapist: I want to take a moment and point out what I think might be happening here. I have the feeling you might disagree with me, but I ask you to listen to what I say and then to view my ideas as one possibility. You have been presenting yourself as inferior and inadequate, a loser, as you call it. You have presented a number of reasons why you think this is so. Regarding this, there are two phenomena I want you to consider. The first is that you seem to be doing everything possible to get me to believe that negative view of yourself. You are arguing with me vigorously, and you seem to be trying to force me to feel that way. The second is that you then act as if I have accepted that view of you, although I haven't said anything indicating that.

Another patient, whenever he experienced intense anxiety, embarrassment, or shame, acted overtly to the therapist to try to make him feel uncomfortable. Thus, he tried to project his image of himself (anxious, shameful, and inadequate) onto the therapist. If the therapist became upset, the patient felt better. This went on repetitively in the therapy hours. After responding on a number of occasions, the therapist began to understand what was happening. In the latter phases of therapy, he was able to interpret the projective identification directly to the patient and generalize about the patient's use of that defense.

In one session, the patient spoke of feeling humiliated when his wife showed little patience with his inability to ejaculate. He then rapidly asked the therapist to call his wife and schedule an immediate appointment for her. He began to be more and more demanding about this. He said that if the therapist didn't call immediately, that would mean that he was a lousy doctor and that the patient should stop treatment. It might be noted that the suggestion to call the patient's wife was a direct provocation, as it had been discussed and rejected in the recent past. Here the therapist commented as follows.

Therapist: I guess the feelings you experience when you talk about your wife's response to your difficulty ejaculating are horribly painful. As we've noted on past occasions, when you feel anxious or embarrassed here, you sometimes try to get rid of those feelings by projecting them onto me. In this case, you're doing everything you can to make me feel inadequate as a therapist. If you make me feel inadequate, you feel better. What do you think about this?

A last example is afforded by a patient who frequently presented himself in some sort of predicament where he was actively in need of and soliciting advice. At times he seemed to be begging for a suggestion. On those rare occasions when the therapist responded with some derivative of a suggestion, the patient then felt intruded upon and offended. At one point, the therapist offered the following comment:

Therapist: You act as if you very much want me to respond. You seem to be almost begging for a suggestion. Then when I do respond, you act offended, as if I'm intruding on you.

This direct intervention led to childhood vignettes involving the patient's father, portrayed as not responding at times of need, yet intruding at times when his advice was not welcome. It turned out that, analogous to the way he acted with the therapist, the patient had elicited the "unwanted" comments from his father.

22

INTROJECTS

Borderline patients frequently present themselves in accordance with two pairs of introjects: the victim–aggressor pair and the inferior–superior pair. This has been elaborated by Meissner (1988) as described in Chapter 12. Interventions are utilized noting the occurrence of these introjects, their pairing, and the shifts from one introject to another. Identification and delineation of each introject come first. Meissner feels that it is easier to identify and delineate the inferior introject before the superior. Likewise, it is easier to delineate the victim introject before the aggressor. Ultimately, the complementary relationship of the pairs needs to be noted and understood.

Interventions regarding any of these introjects are usually ego-dystonic. They are generally resented, rejected, or defended against in various ways. Thus, preparatory comments, as presented in Chapter 18, are useful here. Initially, the therapist should describe the introjective pairs in benign descriptive terms; later he can label using Meissner's terminology.

A patient, a psychologist by profession, chronically saw

herself as being short-changed. She had heavier caseloads and more difficult patients than her colleagues. She didn't get adequate supervision, and she was assigned the worst possible office. She had to work long hours for low pay. Additionally, her husband made little money, necessitating her working even harder. After hearing presentations like this for months, the therapist began to address this victimized stance in a very delicate way.

> *Therapist:* It's very clear that you work exceptionally hard for low pay. It's also clear that your working conditions are far from ideal. Certainly you could benefit from more supervision. Despite the reality of what you say, there's something about the way you say it that I'd like to address. You sometimes present yourself as if you're disadvantaged. Others seem to have it easier and better. What do you think about that?
>
> *Patient:* (angrily) You don't know what it's like. I've had to work hard all my life! You just don't understand!

After many analogous interventions, the patient began to consider what the therapist was saying.

> *Patient:* I'm beginning to see what you mean. I do overwork, and others get better deals, but you're right, I always feel disadvantaged. It's like I'm the victim. But I am the victim! It's been that way all my life. Still I see your point. I take on that role so easily, even when it might not be warranted.

An example of helping a patient to identify an introject of inferiority was presented in Chapter 19 on interventions regarding anxiety and defense. This vignette involves a young man with numerous hospitalizations for suicidal ideation. In this example, the introject of inferiority was both identified and noted to occur as a defense against anxiety.

> *Therapist:* So we see that, again, whenever there is a need to move forward, you become overwhelmed with anxiety. Your

> response to that anxiety is to invoke what we call "the little self image." It's easier to think of yourself as incapable than to move forward in the face of the anxiety you experience.

An example of an intervention late in the therapy, pointing out the pairing of superior and inferior introjects, was presented in Chapter 21 in the section on primitive idealization and devaluation.

> *Therapist:* When you calmly state, as if it's a fact, that your wife is not curious about things and that she won't consider any change whatsoever, you convey the impression that you view her as an inferior person. At that moment, you view yourself as superior and your wife as inferior.

A common occurrence is for a patient to feel victimized while he simultaneously acts the role of aggressor toward the therapist. This often occurs in projective identification.

A patient, whenever he felt rejected or slighted by the therapist, attacked the therapist, accusing him of being unworthy, unreasonable, and demeaning. He felt victimized by the therapist, at the same time that the therapist felt victimized by him. In time, the therapist was able to address this pattern with the patient.

> *Patient:* I just think that you're not a very good therapist. You don't seem genuinely concerned about me. You never display any warmth. And you're so critical.

The therapist was first able to explore with the patient what led to his negative feelings toward him. Then he made the following intervention.

> *Therapist:* We now understand why you feel so negative toward me. You feel that I was harsh and critical last session; you actually experienced me as scolding you. In essence you felt victimized by me. Now let me try to explain something. In

response to feeling victimized, I think that you actually became very harsh and critical of me. And since I had no inkling why, I felt victimized by you. So what I'm hypothesizing is that when you felt victimized by me, in response to that, you acted in a way that actually victimized me.

23

REALITY TESTING

Reality testing, in the structured setting and in day-to-day functioning, is basically intact in the borderline patient. However, many borderline individuals have a tendency toward reversible regressions in reality testing under stress. Under the stress of the intense transference, there is a tendency to distort the therapist's interventions. Because of this, the patient's understanding of the therapist's interventions needs to be regularly examined and clarified. This has been discussed under Input from Patients regarding Interventions in Chapter 18. More flagrant regressions in reality testing during the therapy hours often are best countered by active clarification of reality. In contrast to more psychotic patients, borderline individuals easily accept these interventions, enabling psychotherapeutic exploration to continue.

A patient was suspicious and quite bothered by the prospect that the therapist was recording the session with a tape recorder in his briefcase. When the therapist simply stated that this was not the case, adding that he would never tape the session without obtaining her permission, she accepted the comment and was totally satisfied.

By contrast, a more paranoid patient entertained the same suspicion. In this case, the therapist's clarifying comments meant nothing. When the therapist emptied his briefcase and demonstrated no tape recorder, the patient thought the recorder might be elsewhere in the room. When a search of the office revealed no recorder, the patient claimed it was in the walls. Had the walls been taken apart without finding the recorder, the patient might have claimed it was microscopic.

Another example is provided by Ms. A, on her initial consultation. As she walked in the door, Ms. A stated, "Either you or Dr. B is a liar." She went on to explain that Dr. B had said that I had told him that I would be available for consultation the previous week, yet I told her that I had no time until now. She then demanded to know which one of us was lying. When I explained to her that I had told Dr. B that I had time on Tuesday the earlier week, but that she had not called me until Wednesday, she seemed totally satisfied, calmed down, and related the reason for the consultation.

OFFERING ALTERNATE PERSPECTIVES

Subtle clarifications of reality, in the form of offering alternate possibilities or perspectives of the patient's view of himself, others, and/or the external world, are useful with some borderline patients. When the patient presented in the first example in Chapter 19 portrayed himself as inadequate and inept, grossly failing to live up to his potential, basically being a failure in life, the therapist offered an alternative perspective. Although the patient was certainly not totally living up to his potential, it could be argued that he was moving in a positive direction, doing much better than several years earlier. The fact that he lived alone, had a job for the first time in ten years, and had a girlfriend, could lead to this latter perspective. It was further noted that the patient's portrayal of himself as inadequate and inept occurred at times when he had intense anxiety about moving ahead. Presenting an alternate possibility here confronted the patient's subtle problem in reality testing, expressed by his actually believing his self presentation. The intervention involved a suggestion (that he consider an alternative perspective), and a clarification (that he altered his self representation with anxiety).

A SUPPORTIVE APPROACH WITH PARANOID PATIENTS

In more paranoid patients with selective problems in reality testing, a supportive, nontransference-related dynamic approach can be utilized. Most patients in this category are more psychotic than borderline. I will present an example of a patient whose chief complaint was homosexual innuendoes (Goldstein 1981).

Mr. B was a 34-year-old married man, the father of three children, successfully employed for a number of years as a truck driver. He came for psychotherapy with the chief complaint that innuendoes were going around suggesting that he was homosexual. These innuendoes were conveyed to him by various subtleties, such as someone's putting his finger on his eyebrow, staring at Mr. B's groin area, or motioning to Mr. B in a certain manner. On several occasions, Mr. B became quite upset by the intimations and got into fist fights. The innuendoes had been bothering Mr. B for three months, during which time he also had recurrent obsessive thoughts that others thought he was homosexual. Except during the episodes of fighting, Mr. B kept his ideas of the allusions to himself. He had no idea why people would want to convey these suggestions to him.

Mr. B was a large, muscular man, very athletic, a weight lifter for years. He got along well with his co-workers but suffered from recurrent thoughts that others might not like him. He devoted a lot of time to his family, and was fond of both his wife and children. Sexual relations with his wife were sporadic and characterized by occasional impotency and premature ejaculation. When Mr. B did not perform up to his expectations sexually, he became anxious and depressed. Mr. B had a history, in the last 5 years, of secret heterosexual affairs, in which he performed quite adequately. Mr. B had no history of either homosexuality or of paranoid ideation until the present episode.

I have had some success with a supportive approach as outlined below with several patients very similar to Mr. B. The approach is as follows.

1. Support certain defenses (such as reaction formations) against the unconscious homosexual impulses as they are expressed in the everyday life of the patient.
2. Establish (simultaneously with step 1) that there is an area of vulnerability in the patient. In this case, it is a sensitivity in the area of homosexuality.
3. Help the patient control his impulses in the area of vulnerability (related to the projection of unconscious homosexuality) by:
   a. Limit-setting,
   b. Supporting secondary-process modes of behavior (such as delay, thinking, and talking), and
   c. Supporting obsessional defenses (such as pondering, ruminating, examining all possibilities, etc.)
4. Initiate reality testing in the area of vulnerability, as it occurs in day-to-day life, on a repetitive basis.
5. Identify the external stresses that are related to the area of vulnerability (i.e., that activate the patient's unconscious homosexuality), and help the patient to deal more effectively with these stresses.

Therapy with Mr. B was conducted in accordance with the above outline. The numbers below correspond to those of the outline.

1. Much support was given to Mr. B to assure him that, indeed, he was not homosexual, as evidenced by his muscular appearance, his proclivity for sports, his string of affairs with women, and the fact that he had never had an overt homosexual experience. Thus, the reaction formations used by the patient in everyday life to prove to himself that he was not homosexual were supported and were used as evidence to reinforce for Mr. B that, despite the innuendoes, he, indeed, was not homosexual.
2. The following contradiction was pointed out to Mr. B. On the one hand, he clearly was not homosexual; yet, on the other, he was constantly being disturbed by homosexual innuendoes. He even suffered from recurring thoughts questioning his sexuality. Could it be that he, for some reason, was sensitive and vulnerable to the idea that he might be homosexual? Mr. B latched onto this concept willingly and happily. It was like a revelation to him. Other patients are not so readily responsive here. With most, it is helpful, if possible, to find some data from the patient's early life to help explain and establish his vulnerability.
3. Once the patient accepts the idea that he is vulnerable in this area and has established some therapeutic alliance with the therapist, limit-setting is usually initiated easily. Mr. B was encouraged not to act on the homosexual innuendoes. Reminding him again of his vulnerability in this area, he was asked if it might not be useful to delay action and to talk in psychotherapy instead. Would it not be more helpful to consider all the different possibilities about why, for example, someone rubbed his eyebrow, to ponder about this

action at length, to ruminate over it, rather than to conclude immediately that it was a homosexual innuendo? At all costs, Mr. B should delay acting until he had a chance to talk in his therapy hours.

4. Mr. B was asked if his sensitivity in this area might not lead him to relate other people's actions to his own area of conflict. Being sensitive, might he not tend to personalize? When faced with an area of ambiguity, might he not think too rapidly in terms of homosexual innuendoes? What other possibilities were there?

With each occurrence of what Mr. B perceived as a homosexual innuendo, he brought into the psychotherapy a detailed account of what actually transpired. With a repetitive examination of the details, it was easy to focus on the area of ambiguity and to help show Mr. B how he so often latched prematurely onto explanations involving homosexual innuendoes. With repetitive reality testing, Mr. B became increasingly able to see his distortions and to make adaptations in his area.

With each instance of what Mr. B perceived as a homosexual innuendo, he was actually projecting his own unconscious homosexuality. He was stimulated homosexually but only experienced this urge consciously in the projected form. Since the acknowledgment of his own homosexuality was thought to be too threatening to Mr. B, no effort was made to focus directly on this mechanism of projection of the unconscious homosexuality. Instead, whenever Mr. B was stimulated homosexually, the focus was directed to how Mr. B, in fact, perceived that impulse. Focus was directed to his distortion of reality, to the innuendo, to a discussion of alternative interpretations of the innuendo, and to his vulnerability and sensitivity in that area.

Mr. B did not talk about homosexual innuendoes

regarding the therapist. If he had, the same therapeutic techniques just described would have been used in the here and now with the therapist. That is, the focus with the therapist would have been directed to the innuendo, to a discussion of alternative interpretations of whatever led to the innuendo, to the patient's sensitivity and vulnerability in that area, and to reality testing of what was actually happening in the here and now with the therapist. Additionally, the patient would have been encouraged strongly to bring directly into the therapy all subsequent allusions regarding the therapist.

5. The final step in the psychotherapy was to help Mr. B to understand which external events and life stresses made him particularly prone to think in terms of homosexual innuendoes. These life stresses often involve the patient's inadequate sense of his manliness or masculinity. If the patient's already precarious sense of masculinity is threatened further, unconscious homosexual impulses often surface more easily. Thus, common occurrences that might contribute to the patient's thinking in terms of homosexual innuendoes are rejections by women, difficulties in sexual performance, slights by men at work, poor performance by the patient at masculine pursuits (such as athletics), jokes by others about some aspect of the patient's physical appearance, and so on. These kinds of stresses, along with physical closeness with other men and direct unconscious attraction to other men, are often most troublesome to the patient.

    The goal in such instances is to help the patient link the specific life stresses and his area of vulnerability. By repetitive detailed examination of the occurrences and life circumstances surrounding the events that led the patient to think in terms of homosexual innuendoes, as outlined in step 4, the patient can begin to see that the stresses to which he is vulnerable are specific ones. In other words, he can link certain specific life events to his tendency to think in terms of homosexual innuendoes. Then, via the psychotherapeutic work, he can gradually learn to guard against his propensity to distort when these stresses occur. He can learn to think of these stresses as danger signals and to become rapidly in tune with his proclivity to distort at times of danger.

In the case of Mr. B, three major areas caused him difficulty: inadequate sexual performance with his wife, being the subject of jokes about his muscular physique, and rejections in his pursuit of extramarital affairs. Mr. B learned, whenever he exposed himself to one of these three major areas of danger, to think immediately about his sensitivity and to be on guard against ensuing distortions.

24

PHASES, TRENDS, AND TERMINATION

DEFINITIVE TRENDS OF PSYCHOTHERAPY

Rather than emphasizing specific phases of psychotherapy, I prefer to think in terms of definitive trends as the therapy unfolds. As noted in Chapter 17, the typical borderline patient has a major problem in forming and maintaining a therapeutic alliance. The early work of the therapy invariably focuses on strengthening the alliance. Meaningful interventions regarding core difficulties other than those related to the disrupted alliance can only take place when there is a reasonable therapeutic alliance. There are typically oscillations in the therapy, as described in Chapter 14, between focus on the therapeutic alliance and interventions regarding other core difficulties. One trend in a favorable psychotherapy is for the therapeutic alliance to become gradually and incrementally strengthened, allowing more and more focus on the other core difficulties.

With one group of borderline patients, these other core difficulties are worked through and resolved within the transference. With another group, they are mainly worked through and resolved outside the transference. The first group uses a modified analytically oriented approach throughout the course of psychotherapy. The second group starts with a modified analytically oriented approach and then after the establishment of a reasonable therapeutic alliance, switches to a dynamically oriented modality.

Thus, there are two definitive trends in the psychotherapy with borderline patients. The first, applicable to most borderline patients, is the gradual strengthening of the therapeutic alliance, allowing more focus on the other core difficulties. The second, applicable to a subgroup of borderline patients, is the shift from modified analytically oriented psychotherapy to a dynamically oriented approach. Regardless of approach, it is the repetitive focus on the core difficulties, as they present themselves within and without the transference, together with the repetitive focus on the dynamics regarding the disruptive therapeutic alliance, that leads to gradual understanding and resolution of the core problems. It is this repetitive focus that constitutes the bulk of the psychotherapy.

TERMINATION

Termination can be an exceptionally difficult process for many borderline patients, demanding focus on issues with which these patients are exquisitely sensitive and vulnerable: separation, abandonment, and loss. As these themes are faced and explored in the termination phase, regression and acting out are to be expected. For those patients who are able, it is best to maintain the regularly scheduled appointments, using the termination time to work through these very difficult issues. For some patients, however, this is not reasonable. Flexibility at this stage, with regard to scheduling, to dealing with regressed and acting-out behavior, and with regard to changes in termination plans, is important.

Some borderline patients find the termination issues too painful to deal with and avoid them at all costs. Thus, there can be blanket denial or flights into health. Precipitous premature terminations to avoid uncomfortable feelings are not unusual. Finding it easier to leave a negative situation than to deal with the pain of loss, some patients try to precipitate fights with the therapist, or to fault and devalue the therapist or therapy.

It is useful to set the termination date a number of months in advance. If the date approaches and the patient does not seem "ready" to terminate, it can be pushed forward. With some patients, tapering the frequency of the sessions can make the process more tolerable, helping to decrease regression and acting out. As termination approaches, it is useful for the therapist to tell the patient that he will be available on occasions of need, time and circumstances permitting. The patient is left with an invitation both to consult the therapist at times of stress and to come back for a further course of psychotherapy should the desire arise.

References

Abend, S., Porder, M., and Willick, M. (1983). *Borderline Patients: Psychoanalytic Perspectives.* New York: International Universities Press.

Adler, G. (1981). The borderline-narcissistic personality disorder continuum. *American Journal of Psychiatry* 138:46–50.

——— (1985). *Borderline Psychopathology and Its Treatment.* New York: Jason Aronson.

——— (1993). The psychotherapy of core borderline psychopathology. *American Journal of Psychotherapy* 47(2):194–205.

Adler, G., and Buie, D. (1979). Aloneness and borderline psychopathology: the possible relevance of child development issues. *International Journal of Psycho-Analysis* 60:83–96.

Akhtar, S. (1991). Letter to the editor. *American Journal of Psychiatry* 148(10):1407–1408.

American Psychiatric Association. (1987). *Diagnostic and Statistical Manual of Mental Disorders,* Third Edition-Revised. Washington, DC: American Psychiatric Association.

——— (1994). *Diagnostic and Statistical Manual of Mental Disorders,* Fourth Edition. Washington, DC: American Psychiatric Association.

Bellak, L. (1958). *Schizophrenia: A Review of the Syndrome.* New York: Logos.

Beres, D. (1956). Ego deviation and the concept of schizophrenia. *Psychoan-*

alytic Study of the Child 2:164–235. New York: International Universities Press.

Bibring, E. (1954). Psychoanalysis and the dynamic psychotherapies. *Journal of the American Psychoanalytic Association* 2:745–770.

Bion, W. (1959a). *Experiences in Groups.* New York: Basic Books.

_____ (1959b). Attacks on linking. *International Journal of Psycho-Analysis* 40:308–315.

_____ (1967). *Second Thoughts: Selected Papers on Psychoanalysis.* New York: Basic Books.

Boesky, D. (1983). The problem of mental representation in self and object theory. *Psychoanalytic Quarterly* 52:564–583.

Boyer, L., and Giovacchini, P. (1967). *Psychoanalytic Treatment of Characterological and Schizophrenic Disorders.* New York: Jason Aronson.

Buie, D., and Adler, G. (1982–1983). Definitive treatment of the borderline personality. *International Journal of Psychoanalytic Psychotherapy* 9:51–87.

Bychowsky, G. (1953). The problem of latent psychosis. *Journal of the American Psychoanalytic Association* 4:484–503.

Chessick, R. (1977). *Intensive Psychotherapy of the Borderline Patient.* New York: Jason Aronson.

_____ (1993). The outpatient psychotherapy of the borderline patient. *American Journal of Psychotherapy* 47(2):206–227.

Cohen, M., Baker, G., Cohen, R., et al. (1954). An intensive study of twelve cases of manic-depressive psychosis. *Psychiatry* 17:103–137.

Deutsch, H. (1942). Some forms of emotional disturbance and their relation to schizophrenia. *Psychoanalytic Quarterly* 11:301–321.

Dewald, P. (1971). *Psychotherapy: A Dynamic Approach.* New York: Basic Books.

Dunaif, S., and Hoch, P. (1955). Pseudopsychopathic schizophrenia. In *Psychiatry and the Law,* ed. P. Hoch and J. Zubin. New York: Grune & Stratton.

Fraiberg, S. (1969). Libidinal object constancy and mental representation. *Psychoanalytic Study of the Child* 24:9–47. New York: International Universities Press.

Frosch, J. (1964). The psychotic character: clinical psychiatric considerations. *Psychiatric Quarterly* 38:81–96.

_____ (1970). Psychoanalytic considerations of the psychotic character. *Journal of the American Psychoanalytic Association* 18:24–50.

Gabbard, G. O., and Wilkinson, S. (1994). *Management of Countertransference with Borderline Patients.* Washington, DC: American Psychiatric Press.

Gill, M. (1954). Psychoanalysis and exploratory psychotherapy. *Journal of the American Psychoanalytic Association* 2:771–797.

Giovacchini, P. (1984). *Character Disorders and Adaptative Mechanisms.* New York: Jason Aronson.

_____ (1993a). *Borderline Patients, the Psychosomatic Focus, and the Therapeutic Process.* Northvale, NJ: Jason Aronson.

_____ (1993b). Treatment issues with borderline patients and the psychosomatic focus. *American Journal of Psychotherapy* 47(2):228–244.

Gitelson, M. (1958). On ego distortions. *International Journal of Psycho-Analysis* 39:243–257.

Glover, E. (1931). The therapeutic effect of inexact interpretations: a contribution to the theory of suggestion. *International Journal of Psycho-Analysis* 12:397–411.

Goldstein, W. (1981). A short-term ego supportive treatment approach for the paranoid patient. *Journal: The National Association of Private Psychiatric Hospitals* 12(3):124–127.

_____ (1982). Understanding Kernberg on the borderline patient. *Journal: The National Association of Private Psychiatric Hospitals* 13(1):21–26.

_____ (1983). *DSM-III* and the diagnosis of borderline. *American Journal of Psychotherapy* 37:312–327.

_____ (1985). *An Introduction to the Borderline Conditions.* Northvale, NJ: Jason Aronson.

_____ (1987). Current dynamic thinking regarding the diagnosis of the borderline patient. *American Journal of Psychotherapy* 41(1):4–22.

_____ (1988a). Beginning psychotherapy with the borderline patient. *American Journal of Psychotherapy* 42(4):561–573.

_____ (1988b). Kernberg on the borderline: a simplified version. In *New Concepts of Psychoanalytic Psychotherapy,* ed. J. Ross and W. Meyers, pp. 168–188. Washington, DC: American Psychiatric Press.

_____ (1988c). The depressive impulse-ridden character and the core borderline personality. *American Journal of Psychotherapy* 42(1):28–39.

_____ (1989a). An integration of the views of Kernberg and Adler on borderline pathology. *Bulletin of the Menninger Clinic* 53(4):300–309.

_____ (1989b). Update on psychodynamic thinking regarding the diagnosis of the borderline patient. *American Journal of Psychotherapy* 43(3):321–342.

_____ (1991). Clarification of projective identification. *American Journal of Psychotherapy* 148(2):153–161.

_____ (1992). Book review: *The Fate of Borderline Patients: Successful Outcome and Psychiatric Practice* by Michael Stone. *American Journal of Psychotherapy* 46(1):144–146.

_____ (1994). Book review: *Borderline Patients, the Psychosomatic Focus, and the Therapeutic Process* by Peter Giovacchini. *American Journal of Psychotherapy* 48(2):303–305.

_____ (1995). The borderline patient: update on the diagnosis, theory, and treatment from a psychodynamic perspective. *American Journal of Psychotherapy* 49(3):317–337.

Gray, P. (1994). *The Ego and Analysis of Defense.* Northvale, NJ: Jason Aronson.

Grinker, R. (1975). Neurosis, psychosis, and borderline states. In *Comprehensive Textbook of Psychiatry,* ed. A. Freedman, H. Kaplan, and B. Sadock, pp. 845–850. Baltimore: Williams & Wilkins.

Grotstein, J. (1981). *Splitting and Projective Identification.* New York: Jason Aronson.

Gunderson, J. (1984). *Borderline Personality Disorder.* Washington, DC: American Psychiatric Press.

Gunderson, J., Carpenter, W., and Strauss, J. (1975). Borderline and schizophrenic patients: a comprehensive study. *American Journal of Psychiatry* 132:1257–1264.

Gunderson, J., and Kolb, J. (1978). Discriminating features of borderline patients. *American Journal of Psychiatry* 135:792–796.

Gunderson, J., and Singer, M. (1975). Defining borderline patients: an overview. *American Journal of Psychiatry* 132:1–10.

Hamilton, N. G. (1986). Positive projective identification. *International Journal of Psycho-Analysis* 67:489–496.

_____ (1988). *Self and Others: Object Relations Theory in Practice.* Northvale, NJ: Jason Aronson.

Herman, J., Perry, J., and van der Kolk, B. (1989). Childhood trauma in borderline personality disorder. *American Journal of Psychiatry* 145:490–495.

Hoch, P., and Polatin, P. (1949). Pseudoneurotic forms of schizophrenia. *Psychoanalytic Quarterly* 23:248–276.

Jacobson, E. (1964). *The Self and the Object World.* New York: International Universities Press.

Kernberg, O. (1966). Structural derivatives of object relations. *International Journal of Psycho-Analysis* 47:236–253.

_____ (1967). Borderline personality organization. *Journal of the American Psychoanalytic Association* 15:641–685.

_____ (1968). The treatment of patients with borderline personality organization. *International Journal of Psycho-Analysis* 49:600–619.

_____ (1970). Factors in the treatment of narcissistic personality disorder. *Journal of the American Psychoanalytic Association* 18:51–85.

_____ (1971). A psychoanalytic classification of character pathology. *Journal of the American Psychoanalytic Association* 18:800–821.

_____ (1974). Further contributions to the treatment of narcissistic personalities. *International Journal of Psycho-Analysis* 55:215–240.

_____ (1975). *Borderline Conditions and Pathological Narcissism.* New York: Jason Aronson.

_____ (1976). *Object Relations Theory and Clinical Psychoanalysis.* New York: Jason Aronson.

_____ (1978). Contrasting approaches to the psychotherapy of borderline conditions. In *New Perspectives of Psychotherapy of the Borderline Adult,* ed. J. F. Masterson, pp. 77–104. New York: Brunner/Mazel.

_____ (1980). *Internal World and External Reality.* New York: Jason Aronson.

_____ (1981). Structural interviewing. In *The Psychiatric Clinics of North America: Symposium on Borderline Disorders,* pp. 169–195. Philadelphia: Saunders.

_____ (1982). The psychotherapeutic treatment of borderline personalities. In *Psychiatry 1982: The American Psychiatric Association Annual Review,* ed. L. Grinspoon, pp. 470–487. Washington, DC: American Psychiatric Press.

_____ (1984). *Severe Personality Disorders.* New Haven: Yale University Press.

_____ (1987a). Projection and projective identification: developmental and clinical aspects, in *Projection, Identification, and Projective Identification,* ed. J. Sandler, pp. 93–115. Madison, CT: International Universities Press.

_____ (1987b). Projection and projective identification: developmental and clinical aspects. *Journal of the American Psychoanalytic Association* 35:795–819.

Kernberg, O., Seltzer, M., Koenigsberg, H., et al. (1989). *Psychodynamic Psychotherapy of Borderline Patients.* New York: Basic Books.

Klein, M. (1946). Notes on some schizoid mechanisms. *International Journal of Psycho-Analysis* 27:99–110.

Knight, R. (1953). Borderline states. *Bulletin of the Menninger Clinic* 17:1–12.

Kohut, H. (1966). Forms and transformations of narcissism. *Journal of the American Psychoanalytic Association* 14:243–272.

_____ (1968). The psychoanalytic treatment of narcissistic personality disorders. *Psychoanalytic Study of the Child* 23:86–113. New York: International Universities Press.

_____ (1971). *The Analysis of the Self.* New York: International Universities Press.

_____ (1977). *The Restoration of the Self.* New York: International Universities Press.

_____ (1984). *How Does Analysis Cure?,* ed. A. Goldberg with P. Stepansky. Chicago: University of Chicago Press.

Lichtenberg, J. (1983). *Psychoanalysis and Infant Research.* Hillsdale, NJ: Analytic Press.

Liebowitz, M., and Klein, D. (1981). Interrelationship of hysteroid dysphoria and borderline personality disorder. In *The Psychiatric Clinics of North America: Symposium on Borderline Disorders,* ed. M. Stone, pp. 67–89. Philadelphia: Saunders.

Mahler, M., Pine, F., and Bergman, A. (1975). *The Psychological Birth of the Human Infant.* New York: Basic Books.

Malin, A., and Grotstein, J. (1966). Projective identification in the therapeutic process. *International Journal of Psycho-Analysis* 47:26–31.

Masterson, J. (1976). *Psychotherapy of the Borderline Adult: A Developmental Approach.* New York: Brunner/Mazel.

_____ (1978). *New Perspectives on Psychotherapy of the Borderline Adult.* New York: Brunner/Mazel.

_____, in collaboration with J. Costello. (1980). *From Borderline Adolescent to Functioning Adult: The Test of Time.* New York: Brunner/Mazel.

_____ (1981). *The Narcissistic and Borderline Disorders: An Integrated Developmental Approach.* New York: Brunner/Mazel.

McDevitt, J. (1975). Separation-individuation and object constancy. *Journal of the American Psychoanalytic Association* 23:713–742.

McGlashan, T. (1985). The prediction of outcome in borderline personality disorder: part V of the Chestnut Lodge Follow-up Study. In *The Borderline: Current Empirical Research,* ed. T. McGlashan, pp. 63–98. Washington, DC: American Psychiatric Association.

_____ (1986). Long-term outcome of borderline personalities: part III of The Chestnut Lodge Follow-up Study. *Archives of General Psychiatry* 43:20–30.

Meissner, W. (1980). A note on projective identification. *Journal of the American Psychoanalytic Association* 28:43–67.

_____ (1982–1983). Notes on the potential differentiation of borderline conditions. *International Journal of Psychoanalytic Psychotherapy* 9:3–49.

_____ (1983). Notes on the levels of differentiation within borderline conditions. *Psychoanalytic Review* 70:179–209.

_____ (1984). *The Borderline Spectrum: Differential Diagnosis and Developmental Issues.* New York: Jason Aronson.

_____ (1988). *Treatment of Patients in the Borderline Spectrum.* Northvale, NJ: Jason Aronson.

_____ (1993). Treatment of patients in the borderline spectrum: an overview. *American Journal of Psychotherapy* 47(2):184–193.

Ogata, S., Silk, K., Goodrich, S., et al. (1990). Childhood sexual and physical abuse in adult patients with borderline personality disorder. *American Journal of Psychiatry* 147:1009–1013.

Ogden, T. (1979). On projective identification. *International Journal of Psycho-Analysis* 60:357–373.

_____ (1982). *Projective Identification and Psychotherapeutic Technique.* New York: Jason Aronson.

_____ (1986). *The Matrix of the Mind: Object Relations and the Psychoanalytic Dialogue.* Northvale, NJ: Jason Aronson.

Perry J., and Klerman, G. (1978). The borderline patient. *Archives of General Psychiatry* 35:141–150.

_____ (1980). Clinical features of the borderline personality. *American Journal of Psychiatry* 137:165–173.

Piaget, J. (1954). *The Construction of Reality in the Child,* trans. by M. Cook. New York: Basic Books, 1937.

Porder, M. (1987). Projective identification: an alternative hypothesis. *Psychoanalytic Quarterly* 56:431–451.

Racker, H. (1957). The meanings and uses of countertransference. *Psychoanalytic Quarterly* 26:303–357.

_____ (1968). *Transference and Countertransference.* New York: International Universities Press.

Ramchandani, D. (1991). Letter to the editor. *American Journal of Psychiatry* 148(10):1409.

Rapaport, D., Gill, M., and Schafer, R. (1945–1946). *Diagnostic Psychological Testing.* Chicago: Year Book.

Rinsley, D. (1977). An object relations view of the borderline personality. In *Borderline Personality Disorders: The Concept, the Syndrome, the Patient,* ed. P. Hartocollis, pp. 47–70. New York: International Universities Press.

——— (1978). Borderline psychopathology: a review of etiology, dynamics, and treatment. *International Review of Psycho-Analysis* 5:45.

——— (1982). *Borderline and Other Self Disorders: A Developmental and Object Relations Perspective.* New York: Jason Aronson.

——— (1989). *Developmental Pathogenesis and Treatment of Borderline and Narcissistic Personalities.* Northvale, NJ: Jason Aronson.

Rockland, L. (1989). *Supportive Therapy: A Psychodynamic Approach.* New York: Basic Books.

——— (1992). *Supportive Therapy for Borderline Patients: A Psychodynamic Approach.* New York: Guilford.

Rosenfeld, H. (1952). Notes on the psycho-analysis of the superego conflict of an acute schizophrenic patient. *International Journal of Psycho-Analysis* 33:111–131.

——— (1954). Considerations regarding the psycho-analytic approach to acute and chronic schizophrenia. *International Journal of Psycho-Analysis* 35:135–140.

——— (1965). *Psychotic States: A Psychoanalytic Approach.* New York: International Universities Press.

Sandler, J. (1987). The concept of projective identification. In *Projection, Identification, and Projective Identification,* pp. 13–26. Madison, CT: International Universities Press.

Sandler, J., and Rosenblatt, B. (1960). The concept of the representational world. *Psychoanalytic Study of the Child* 17:128–145. New York: International Universities Press.

Schaffer, N. (1986). The borderline patient and affirmative interpretation. *Bulletin of the Menninger Clinic* 50:148–162.

Segal, H. (1964). *Introduction to the Work of Melanie Klein.* New York: Basic Books.

Shapiro, E., Shapiro, R., Zinner, J., et al. (1977). The borderline-ego and the working alliance: indications for family and individual treatment in adolescence. *International Journal of Psycho-Analysis* 58:77–89.

Spitz, R. (1965). *The First Year of Life: A Psychoanalytic Study of Normal and*

Deviant Development of Object Relations. New York: International Universities Press.

Spitzer, R., Endicott, J., and Gibbon, M. (1979). Crossing the border into borderline personality and borderline schizophrenia. *Archives of General Psychiatry* 36:17–24.

Stern, A. (1938). Psychoanalytic investigation and therapy in the borderline group of neurosis. *Psychoanalytic Quarterly* 7:467–489.

Stern, D. (1985). *The Interpersonal World of the Infant: A View from Psychoanalysis and Developmental Psychology.* New York: Basic Books.

Stone, L. (1951). Psychoanalysis and brief psychotherapy. *Psychoanalytic Quarterly* 20:215–236.

_____ (1954). The widening scope of indications for psychoanalysis. *Journal of the American Psychoanalytic Association* 2:567–594.

_____ (1986). Psychoanalytic observations on the pathology of depressive illness: selected spheres of ambiguity or disagreement. *Journal of the American Psychoanalytic Association* 34:329–362.

Stone, M. (1987). Systems for defining a borderline case. In *The Borderline Patient: Emerging Concepts in Diagnosis, Psychodynamics, and Treatment,* vol. I, pp. 13–35, ed. J. Grotstein, M. Solomon, and J. Lang. Hillsdale, NJ: Analytic Press.

_____ (1988). Toward a psychobiological theory of the borderline personality disorder: Is irritability the red thread that runs through borderline conditions? *Dissociation* I:1–41.

_____ (1990a). *The Fate of Borderline Patients: Successful Outcome and Psychiatric Practice.* New York: Guilford.

_____ (1990b). Treatment of borderline patients: a pragmatic approach to psychotherapy and psychopharmacology. *Psychiatric Clinics of North America* 13:265–286.

_____ (1993). Paradoxes in the management of suicidability in borderline patients. *American Journal of Psychotherapy* 47(2):255–272.

Tarachow, S. (1963). *An Introduction to Psychotherapy.* New York: International Universities Press.

Ticho, E. (1970). Differences between psychoanalysis and psychotherapy. *Bulletin of the Menninger Clinic* 34:128–139.

Vaillant, G. (1971). Theoretical hierarchy of adaptive ego mechanisms. *Psychiatry* 24:107–18.

Volkan, V. (1987). *Six Steps in the Treatment of Borderline Personality Organization.* Northvale, NJ: Jason Aronson.

Waldinger, R. (1987). Intensive psychodynamic therapy with borderline patients: an overview. *American Journal of Psychiatry* 144:267–274.

_____ (1993). The role of psychodynamic concepts in the diagnosis of borderline personality disorder. *Harvard Review of Psychiatry* 1:158–167.

Waldinger, R., and Gunderson, J. (1987). *Effective Psychotherapy with Borderline Patients: Case Studies.* New York: Macmillan.

Wallerstein, R. (1965). The goals of psychoanalysis: a survey of analytic viewpoints. In *Psychotherapy and Psychoanalysis: Theory-Practice-Research,* pp. 99–118. New York: International Universities Press.

Winnicott, D. (1953). Transitional objects and transitional phenomena. *International Journal of Psycho-Analysis* 34:89–97.

_____ (1965). Ego distortion in terms of the true and false self. In *The Maturation Processes and the Facilitating Environment,* pp. 140–152. New York: International Universities Press.

Zanarini, M., Gunderson, J., and Marino, M. (1989). Child experiences of borderline patients. *Comprehensive Psychiatry* 30:10–25.

Zetzel E. (1971). The so-called good hysteric. *International Journal of Psycho-Analysis* 49:256–260.

Zilboorg, G. (1941). Ambulatory schizophrenics. *Psychiatry* 4:149–155.

Zinner, J. (1976). The implications of projective identification for marital interaction. In *Contemporary Marriage: Structure, Dynamics, and Therapy,* ed. H. Grunebaum and J. Christ. Boston: Little, Brown.

Zinner, J., and Shapiro, R. (1972). Projective identification as a mode of perception and behavior in families of adolescents. *International Journal of Psycho-Analysis* 53:523–530.

Credits

Chapter 3 is an expanded version of "An Integration of the Views of Kernberg and Adler on Borderline Pathology," published in the *Bulletin of the Menninger Clinic* 53(4):300–309, copyright © 1989, The Menninger Foundation, and is reprinted by permission.

Chapter 5 is an updated version of "Clarification of Projective Identification," published in the *American Journal of Psychiatry* 148(2):153–161, copyright © 1991, the American Psychiatric Association, and is reprinted by permission.

Chapter 6 is a revised version of "The Depressive Impulse-Ridden Character and the Core Borderline Personality," published in the *American Journal of Psychotherapy* 42(1):28–29, copyright © 1988, and is reprinted by permission.

Much of Chapter 7 is taken from "Update on Psychodynamic Thinking regarding the Diagnosis of the Borderline Patient," published in the *American Journal of Psychotherapy* 43(3):321–352, copyright © 1989, and is reprinted by permission.

Index